THE
ENLIGHTENMENT
INTENSIVE

DYAD COMMUNICATION AS A TOOL FOR SELF-REALIZATION

LAWRENCE NOYES

THE

ENLIGHTENMENT

INTENSIVE

DYAD COMMUNICATION AS A TOOL FOR SELF-REALIZATION

LAWRENCE NOYES

Frog, Ltd.
Berkeley, California

Note: Although the information and practices in this book may well be useful for anyone interested in the subject of enlightenment, it is sold with the understanding that neither the author nor the publisher is engaged in presenting specific psychological or spiritual advice to the reader, nor making promises of specific results. Each person has unique psychological and spiritual needs at any given time, and the results in any spiritual practice tend to vary from person to person.

The Enlightenment Intensive:
Dyad Communication as a Tool for Self-Realization

Published by
Frog, Ltd.
Frog, Ltd. books are distributed by
North Atlantic Books
P.O. Box 12327
Berkeley, California 94712

Cover and book design by Nancy Koerner
Photography: pages xv, 2, 28, 53, 56, 68, 79, 85, 102, 119 Winfried Kaiser; pages 8, 10, 20, 36, 47, 62, 66, 92, 180 Goldie Grahame; page 67 Rita Wyser; page 106 Massimo Rossi; page 115 Ralph Granz; page 117 Margrit Hui; page 125 Hunter Bahnson; page 129 Epi van De Pol; page 136 Dawn Riddle; page 139 Norbert Hartmann; page 142 Robert McCarthy; pages 146, 149, 155 L.D. Noyes; page 152 Barry Barankin; page 174 Barbara Szepan.
Printed in the United States of America

Library of Congress Cataloging-in-Publication Data

Noyes, Lawrence.
    The Enlightenment Intensive : dyad communication as a tool for
self-realization / Lawrence Noyes.
        p.   cm.
    Includes index.
    ISBN 1-883319-73-0 (pbk. : alk. paper)
    1. Self-realization. I. Title.
BJ1470.N69 1998
291.4'2--dc21   98-18358
                                                        CIP

1 2 3 4 5 6 7 / 02 01 00 99 98

*With gratitude to all those I have met through this work
who have constantly touched me with the beauty of
who they are,
and filled my life with their wisdom and love.*

TABLE OF CONTENTS

INTRODUCTION

I do not seek to follow in the footsteps of the
men of old. I seek what they sought.
—Basho

IN EARLY JULY OF 1968, out on a canyon property in the high desert east of Los Angeles, twenty-six men and women set out for five days on an audacious experiment in personal growth and self-awakening. They used the ancient meditation practice of contemplating a question such as "Who am I?" or "What is my true nature?" and combined it with the more modern approach of sitting with a partner and communicating what occurs as a result. The aim was not merely to have interesting experiences or to come up with new intellectual answers to these questions; it was to try to break through into enlightenment, the spontaneous awakening of consciousness known in Zen as *kensho* or *satori*. They were going after the real thing, whatever that was. And in this break-the-mold synthesis of East and West, some of them actually succeeded. Their experiment was the birth of what is now known in over twenty countries as the Enlightenment Intensive.

One of the people who succeeded in that first experiment was a thirty-five-year-old Brooklyn man named Yon Kane. Years later, in 1995, Yon sat comfortably by a warm fire in his home in Richmond, California, and described what occurred for him during that time out in the desert:

What happened for me on that first one is that the passion for the truth turned on in me. I was working hard on the question "What is the purpose of life?" I remember lying awake in the middle of the night thinking, "What is it? What is it?!" I was really focused. I was like on a train and all this stuff was going by the windows: thoughts, feelings, images, whatever. But I knew none of that was it. Meanwhile I had this passion for the truth that had just grabbed me, that was driving this train.

The day before, I had gone through a period of real despair, feeling like I had to find more meaning to life than just working at a job and eating. Later I got to another place where I felt that if I asked myself that question one more time I would just die. But I really wanted the truth, so I kept going. Then on the last morning we were doing a sitting contemplation. And suddenly everything disappeared and I went into union. I was in this infinite, timeless experience of union, and it was like no experience I had ever had before. And it no longer mattered what the purpose of life was because the purpose was the union itself that I was experiencing, not some answer.

I was in exquisite ecstasy from this. I would use the word "bliss" now, but I didn't know that word then. For hours, though, every time I touched onto this experience, there were waves of bliss, just waves of it. It was so exquisite, and so unexpected, that I was crying. Later I was laughing from the joy of it all. This continued on throughout the last day.

This is a book about the Enlightenment Intensive, a unique method for transcending the morass of the intellect and directly experiencing into the ultimate reality. In its first three decades, over fifty thousand people took one or more of these Intensives. Not all of them got the kind of result that Yon did. Genuine enlightenment is not something that can be guaranteed. Many of these people, though, after three days of working at their question, went home more in touch with themselves and better able to relate authentically with others. Having drunk deeply of the tonic that is the simple spoken truth, a lot of them experienced a freeing up of new energies for living life on a more real and satisfying basis. Many experienced levels of inner peace and stillness of mind that they had never known. And for some, often around a third of any given group, something even more extraordinary took place: the striking breakthrough into enlightenment.

ENLIGHTENMENT

Enlightenment has been spoken about and written about for a very long time by mystics, religious founders, yogis, Zen masters, and more or less ordinary people who have happened to stumble onto it in the course of their journey through life. Whether in ancient times or modern, there is a consistency in their reports of the special and indescribable nature of the event, the priceless penetrations into reality, the abiding inner peace that remained to some degree afterwards.

Yet in mainstream culture here in the West, there has long been a taboo against serious discussion of what the word 'enlightenment' is really trying to describe. Not many systems have been developed here for coming to experience it. This situation has been changing in recent decades, and the Enlightenment Intensive has been part of that change, but the word 'enlightenment' is still used casually in our language. To this day it can refer to anything from a lecture that someone liked ("It was an enlightening experience") to a rude awakening ("My tax accountant just enlightened me about what I owe this year").

The enlightenment discussed in this book is a unique condition of direct, conscious experience that reveals in an instant of penetration our ultimate nature. This experience goes completely beyond our personality, our body, our problems, and our ideas about ourselves. It is a transformative union of self and truth that is not an insight or even an intuition. Its nature lies outside the realm of our thinking and sensing processes. Yet it is real. And it is the condition that evolves consciousness at the core, revealing the inner splendor of the true self in ways that must be seen and experienced to be appreciated.

On a practical basis, enlightenment has enormous implications for our capacity to achieve a genuine sense of well-being, to face situations on more real terms, to live more from who we really are rather than from our neuroses and upsets. It enables us to conduct spiritual growth in the realm of reality as opposed to the realm of ideas. In many Yogic and Buddhist systems, in fact, the initial awakenings into the realm of enlightenment are even considered the *beginning* of real spiritual practice. Enlightenment may not necessarily teach us how to balance a checkbook or fix a broken bone, but it does clarify what's what at increasingly more basic levels of existence and nonexistence. This opens doors in our consciousness and in our hearts that mere book-learning or sophisticated thinking processes seem wholly unable to open.

About the long-term effects of his enlightenment experience twenty-seven years earlier, Yon told me:

That experience was my first true spiritual awakening. It changed my whole life. The main thing I got from it was a self-confidence about who I am. I became confident at just being who I am, at being able to hold my own with anybody. It gave me a depth to my life that, as far as I can tell, can't be obtained through any other kind of experience. I've had a real appreciation for people since then, too. Even if they don't think they're someone, I do. I still have things happen in my life, and issues come up, but there is a basic happiness I've had since then that never went away. And I know I'm not totally enlightened. I know this happiness could be deeper. But it's deep enough for me now, and it's totally satisfying. I don't have any anxiety about getting more deeply enlightened, either. If I do, okay, and if there are setbacks, okay. I have this basic knowledge of who I am and the nature of life, so there is no anxiety about all that.

PARTNER-ASSISTED MEDITATION

Up until fairly recent times, most time-tested approaches we've had for enlightenment originated in the East, and most have involved a silent, solo meditation approach of one sort or another. On an Enlightenment Intensive, people also contemplate, and are taught how to do so. The difference is that they have a partner sitting there who will listen to whatever they have to say about what has occurred in their contemplation. This is something completely new. As people alternate five-minute turns in the role of the listener, both are more able to journey ahead in their own unique process of self-discovery.

In these dyads, people face all the tricks and demons of the mind that solo meditators throughout history have come to know. These tricks and demons all take place: mind chatter, drowsiness, boredom, doubts, and fears, along with the more pleasant, nonenlightenment aspects such as peacefulness, insights, and empty-mindedness. This inner world is not somehow avoided on the Enlightenment Intensive. But now it can be navigated more easily for many people by virtue of the presence of a listening partner.

This form of partner-assisted meditation in a dyad structure follows a few simple ground-rules, the basics of which can be learned in about twenty minutes. It has an elegant precision and built-in discipline to it, yet it is large-hearted, spacious, and user-friendly. It is very powerful when used in intensive retreat formats.

In late December of 1976, some eight years after that initial experiment, I took my first three-day Enlightenment Intensive near San Francisco. There were about seventy-five of us, people young and old, from all over the United States. By then, the method had been well developed, and we were under the guidance of an experienced staff. Twelve times a day we each chose a new partner and sat down face-to-face in a forty-minute dyad. When it was my turn, I worked on the question "Who am I?" and then communicated to my partner whatever occurred as a result. When it was my partner's turn, I listened silently to the results of his or her contemplation. Our turns were regulated by a cassette-recorded bell that gently sounded throughout the room every five minutes. People were working on either "Who am I?" "What am I?" "What is life?" or "What is another?"

There was a lot about this event I hadn't seen before. I had always thought spiritual retreats took place in monastic-like settings, but here we were in an old community hall in a residential neighborhood of two- and three-story houses. The weather was cool and pleasant. The streets were quiet because it was still the Christmas holidays. Occasionally a young person glided by on a bicycle. Inside, though, a powerful, non-normal process was unfolding, as hour after hour each of us grappled with one of these universal questions, trying to experience its truth directly.

Sitting in the long rows of dyads, I noticed that the personal styles varied widely: some pondered their question wide-eyed and wonderingly; others sat with eyes closed, delving into it's inner mysteries; some attacked their question passionately, as if they were wrestling with the gods above—"WHO AM I?! WHO IS THIS SITTING HERE IN MY SEAT, ASKING THIS QUESTION?!" I thought meditation retreats were tranquil, silent affairs, but here the room hummed and buzzed as we each gnawed on our particular question and shared with our partner whatever came up. In a flowing, vibrant sea of contemplation and sometimes raucous sharing, we charged into our question again and again and embraced it, ran from it, pawed at it, analyzed it, got bored with it, loved it, hated it, and generally went through almost anything you can imagine. With meals, breaks, and lectures to help support us, we returned again and again to the forty-minute dyads, choosing a new partner each time and sitting down again for another run at it.

I remember being relieved at the start to find that there would be no discussion by any staff person about who I am or who I'm not, or what "the truth" is or isn't. There wasn't going to be any philosophy or belief system I would have to take on first in order to get the benefits later. I wasn't going to be emotionally broken down by a powerful seminar leader. Something deep inside of me responded to the fact that here was a self-awakening method run by a knowledgeable staff, and it was up to me to apply it as well as I could, starting right where I was and going forward at my own rate.

A PURE PRACTICE

It was not so easy to categorize what we were doing. Although partially rooted in the ancient Zen *koan* practices and the even older tradition in Yoga of contemplating "Who am I?" the Enlightenment Intensive is not, in itself, a religion, a branch of Zen or Yoga, or a part of any other system. It does not teach a life-encompassing doctrine. It offers, in fact, no grand theories about anything. It is not an organization that people join. It has sometimes been incorporated into organizations by people who recognize its value, but the method itself walks alone. It is, essentially, a pure practice. As such, it is a practical response to the age-old question of seekers everywhere when they have heard about the possibility of enlightenment: How do I get there?

In terms of results, the Enlightenment Intensive has never presumed to match the fully stabilized self-realizations of the great Yoga and Zen masters of old, those legendary spiritual figures who, with years of practice and numerous levels of enlightenment behind them, ultimately shined forth from their true nature in every action and word. How alluring it is to read that they achieved a way of living free of any tendency to fall even briefly from the enlightened state. The Enlightenment Intensive obviously cannot promise that kind of result in a mere three days. Yet it does offer the possibility for a wide range of people to safely explore into the nature of reality and for some to achieve a degree of the direct knowing that enlightened beings throughout the ages have experienced. It is thus a twentieth-century tool for beginning and middle levels of enlightenment that has neither the long, gray beard of Zen or Yoga nor the mountainlike richness of their legacies. But on the other hand, it is now well past the stage of childhood.

At this writing, thirty years have passed since its creation. The Enlightenment Intensive is well tried and tested. Historically, it has moved about mainly by word of mouth. Its natural fuel has always been the heartfelt affection that many people, having participated in one, feel for it.

I am one of those people. I was twenty-five when I took my first Enlightenment Intensive. By that time I had read plenty of books, done lots of thinking and was in fairly serious danger of becoming an intellectual off in his own world. I had a degree in psychology, but it seemed to me that psychology as a whole lacked an assured fix on the real nub of who and what we are apart from our neuroses. I liked books on Zen because the authors spoke with clarity and sureness about this domain of our true nature beyond our life problems. They spoke of the sacred basis of reality as a discoverable actuality. But the lucidness of Zen didn't call me to practice.

In some unformed way, I was looking for a method for me, a regular, late-twentieth-century American guy. I wanted to do my explorations without jumping into an ancient and arduous religious tradition that was foreign to me. I already had some sense of who I am but I wanted a fuller sense, more independent from . . . anything. In short, I wanted to experience more deeply who and what I am, and what life really is. And I used to wonder, "Is this too much to ask, to want to experience these things before I really get on with my life?" I was distracted in school because of this inner wondering and the fact that it was not really being addressed in any way meaningful to me. I wasn't completely satisfied with the church and the psychological systems I had looked into. So I kept looking, keeping my radar up, seeking an approach accessible to me as I am.

The Enlightenment Intensive was a real response to this particular searching of mine. Not everyone takes to this method, but I did. In that three-day effort I worked hard and followed the staff's instructions as well as I could. And lo and behold, at an unexpected moment, I directly experienced the me that I am. The spontaneous breakthrough in consciousness and the union I experienced were of a type I had never heard described in my years of psychological studies. I was briefly in a world far beyond my own neuroses and worries. It was not psychosis or separation from reality, it was the essence of reality, a place before neuroses and worries even enter into the picture.

In one very real sense, though, nothing at all had changed: I was still me. It wasn't as if there were a new me. Yet, something fundamental had changed. My experience of myself at the core was of an authentic place that was my true home in the universe. This was relieving, and centering to the core of my being. In a fell swoop, it cut right through the morass of my social training, childhood issues, and the world of ideas about myself. Looking back now, from a point over twenty years later, what I sensed deeply at the time has been validated by all events since: that a life truer to myself, and the real spiritual work I had to do, began right then and there.

For years now I have seen the Enlightenment Intensive work well for a lot of people, from many different countries. However, no one should think this is a 100 percent-guaranteed process. People get a variety of results. Some people try but just can't get into the method at all. And not everyone breaks through into the unique state of direct experience known as enlightenment, a fact that calls upon people to take a broader and more mature approach to their spiritual enquiry efforts than to expect all good things to happen in a single three-day weekend. So the claim here is not that this is a surefire method for everyone. Yet over the years the Enlightenment Intensive has continued to flourish on the strengths of its own merits. It has taken its place as a tool for self-realization we now have in our culture, a tool not simply for monks but one for people from all walks of life.

This book, then, is an introduction to this inspired method, to what it is and what it isn't, written for anyone honestly seeking a deeper experience of who and what we really are. If you are such a person, one thing this book can do is help you make an informed decision about whether taking an Enlightenment Intensive is something you want to do or not. If you are about to take one, whether it be your first one or not, some portions of this book can help arm you against the tricks of the mind that have caused so many seekers to give up in despair or settle for lesser experiences that fall short of the real thing. Some of the history of Enlightenment

Intensives is also documented here. At a more basic level, this book is a report of findings from the laboratory of the Enlightenment Intensive. It stands on thirty years' experience and speaks of the places I and some others have been in our own searchings for truth and a better life in our times.

BIRTH OF A NEW WAY:
THE EXPERIMENT IN THE DESERT

Beyond this shore and the further shore, beyond the beyond,
where there is no beginning and no end, without fear, go.

—Buddha

WHAT IS AN ENLIGHTENMENT INTENSIVE, and where did it come from? The story begins . . . well, it depends on how far back we want to go. People have been searching into their true nature for thousands of years, some of them succeeding and leaving behind methods and teachings for those of us who come later. But the Enlightenment Intensive is not simply an old system in a new package. It was inspired by known methods from the past, especially *Rinzai Zen*, but it also contains the new element of the dyad form of communication. How this method came into being reveals a lot about what the Enlightenment Intensive is, how it works, and who the kind of people are who will invest themselves in the challenge of trying to directly experience the truth itself.

The story that follows tells this story, and it *is* a story. I myself wasn't there at the beginning. But from interviewing some of the people who were there, a creation account based on their memories can be formed. This is the story of what happened.

In early 1968, the conceptual kernel of what became the Enlightenment Intensive was born in an instant of insight to a thirty-eight-year-old Southern California man named Charles Berner. At the time, he and his wife, Ava, were running a healing and growth center in Costa Mesa. They were offering classes in health, mind studies, and communication training. From working in sessions with clients, Charles had seen again and again that honest communication was one of the key elements for helping people resolve personal problems and realize their hidden potential. He had thus been concentrating his efforts on helping others become more able to express themselves truthfully and appropriately, as well as learn to be good listeners. Ava was interested in all matters to do with health and relating. As a couple involved in the creation of a joint venture, they supported and inspired each other.

THE WESTERN INFLUENCE: THE DYAD

One of the new formats for improving communication that emerged from their work was something they called the dyad. The word comes from the Greek *dyo*, meaning "consisting of two." A dyad is two people seated facing each other, each taking turns listening while the other speaks. Ava had come up with the idea for this kind of dyad work in 1965 as a solution to a certain problem that had developed: people were coming to the center who wanted to participate but they couldn't afford to pay for time in an individual session. In dyad groups, anyone could come for a

nominal fee and, under Charles's or Ava's guidance, pick a partner, sit down in a safe and structured format, and talk honestly to someone who would listen.

In these dyads, one person gave the other a specific instruction, such as "Tell me a problem you are currently having" or "Tell me your goals for life." The partner answered as honestly as he or she could, while the other listened without interrupting. After a prearranged amount of time had passed, the listener acknowledged the speaker by saying, "Thank you." The partners then reversed roles.

People liked dyads, because in them they had the opportunity to freely express themselves on important issues without being interrupted, judged, or having someone else give their own opinion. They were a safe and inexpensive space where the truth could be spoken and received. And they fitted in with the times. The whole atmosphere of the late 1960s was beginning to really hit its stride then. There was a wide-open creativity in the air and a kind of voraciousness to try out fresh ideas and absorb new influences.

THE EASTERN INFLUENCE:
MEDITATION AND ENLIGHTENMENT

Among the influences that began to appear in this high-octane period was that of the ancient spiritual heritage of the East. An influx began of spiritual teachers from India, Tibet, and Japan, who spoke of meditation and mystical states of self-awareness. Such experiences and self-awakenings, they said, led to an inner fulfillment much greater than ordinary life could provide. The wider public, it will be recalled, tended to equate this talk with the lingo of the drug culture, and were suspicious of it. Certainly for a lot of people the study of these Eastern approaches was casual and superficial. But as the whole '60s thing unfolded in all its idealism and flamboyance, some talented researchers, working off center-stage and usually independently, began looking into what these ancient traditions were really trying to get at when they talked about 'enlightenment.'

Charles was one of them. At one point he got ahold of Philip Kapleau's *The Three Pillars of Zen,* a groundbreaking book that came out in 1965 and went on to have a major influence in attracting Westerners to Japanese Zen practice. Other books on Zen philosophy had been around for some years, but *Three Pillars* was comprehensive, spotlighting in detail the meditation practices themselves. In it, Kapleau did an admirable job of introducing Western readers to what enlightenment is and is not, unraveling the words of Buddha that "He who finds it finds nothing. He who finds it finds everything."

As Ava described it years later: "In that period, Charles would sit up in bed at night reading *Three Pillars* and talking it over with me. A lot of his ideas for the Enlightenment Intensive—how to structure it and run it—later came from there. But at the time he was just reading it, looking into the subject."

In the second part of the book, Kapleau gives some accounts of enlightenments that had taken place during what are called the *sesshins*. In Zen practice, *sesshins* are periods lasting five or seven days, sometimes longer, during which the monks live a more intensive lifestyle. The daily schedule includes more meditation periods than usual, and the monastery is energized with a "go for it" atmosphere. The whole intention in these *sesshins* is to break through into some level of enlightenment. *Sesshins* are an old tradition. Before Zen arrived in Japan from China in the period around 1100 A.D., some of the early Chinese Zen masters had established the pattern of going into *sesshin* during the monsoon season. When the heavy rains came, work outside was naturally restricted, and the elements supported an inward turning of concentrated attention.

In *sesshin*, then as now, the monks ardently apply their contemplation practices, called *zazen*. There are a number of variations of *zazen* practice. A common one calls for the monk to contemplate a *koan*, a logically meaningless question such as "What is the sound of one hand clapping?" or "What was my face before my parents were born?" The aim of *koan* practice is enlightenment, which is known in Zen as *kensho* or *satori*. *Kensho* normally refers to the beginning flashes of enlightenment that occur in the earlier stages of practice, and *satori* to the deeper, more stable enlightenments that come later on.

Kapleau includes a number of firsthand accounts of several Americans and a Canadian housewife having recently achieved such enlightenment experiences as a result of *zazen* practice in *sesshins*. These visitors to the Zen monasteries in Japan reported fundamental changes in self-awareness and personal fulfillment at the core. Instead of struggling with life and searching for fulfillment outside of themselves, they now seemed to carry a good measure of it *within them*, wherever they went.

These accounts showed that enlightenment was not a superstitious relic of an ancient and ignorant people. They also showed that modern Westerners could succeed at an Eastern method. This was impressive, especially since Westerners by now were earning a reputation in the ashrams and monasteries of the East for being intelligent and sincere but also restless and spoiled. They usually showed up eager, but also with culture shock, language problems, discipline problems, and intestinal problems. They appeared to be afflicted with strange, modern neuroses not anticipated by any of the known scriptures of old. This all presented problems, and in these traditions that call for years of training and practice, only a tiny percentage of them found a way to settle in for the long haul. The East and its ancient ways were ultimately foreign to the majority of Westerners. What could be done for those living an active lifestyle rooted in the West?

Looking back, it is clear that the East and the West were trying to get to know each other in this period. The West, as a culture, had not been specializing for centuries in contemplation as had the East; it had been specializing in dynamic, outward-oriented interaction and effort. In this context, those working in the therapeutic and growth movement had been discovering the power of honest communication for freeing mental tension, clearing the mind of its chatter, and deepening the awareness of oneself and others. In the corner of the universe in which Charles and Ava worked, the dyads and individual sessions were clearly helping people come out of their shell and relate more effectively. But the whole approach of open relating seemed to be completely at odds with the long hours of silent sitting that Kapleau and others were describing as the absolutely essential tool in enlightenment work. In terms of the growth of consciousness, the exact relationship between silent meditation and relating was emerging as something of a mystery.

By early 1968, Charles had unwittingly become a container for these two very different orientations, a kind of human beaker sitting in the turned up flame of the times. He continued his reading and met with various Zen masters, yogis, and Buddhists who visited Los Angeles. He experimented with meditation techniques himself. Month by month, more information and experience were arriving in his inner world, mixing around in an uneasy concoction. It was uneasy because on the one hand the ancient approaches of the East were unyielding about the need for sustained meditation in silence. They emphasized this mysterious thing called enlightenment rather than mere therapeutic results. On the other hand, Westerners, especially Americans, liked contact and open communication. They liked relating, making progress at resolving problems, and becoming more effective in the world.

THE VALUE OF KNOWING WHO YOU ARE

During this period Charles began to see more clearly that no matter what therapeutic technique or helping approach he used, whether it was dyads, communication skill training, dream work, health maintenance or whatever, the people who had a clear inner sense of who they are tended to benefit rapidly. But the people who were confused or unconscious as to who they are, who were stuck in personality traits or inauthentic behavior, tended, on the other hand, to have a difficult time progressing, no matter what the approach was.

It seemed to Charles that more people would get a lot more out of *any* self-improvement or spiritual technique if they could only have a primary, direct experience of who and what they actually are. With this basic consciousness they could then apply any self-help or spiritual technique and live life right from themselves rather than from a limited role such as "housewife" or "businessman," or from a fixed personality such as "helpless victim" or "tough guy." He started thinking about how this could be done such that modern Westerners, with all their quirks and ways, would readily succeed in a reasonable period of time. He knew that Ramanamaharshi and other yogis had used the question "Who am I?" as a silent contemplation tool. Kapleau too had explained that "Who am I?" and "What am I?" were ancient Zen *koans*, two among the many commonly used by monks over the centuries. These *koans* didn't seem obscure or cast in the style of any single master; they seemed to be universal questions that directed the meditator's attention in a straightforward way into the realm of his or her own true nature.

SYNTHESIS:
THE CONCEPTUAL BREAKTHROUGH

Charles described it years later:

> *What happened was this: I was at a place in the Santa Cruz mountains in California and I had four or five hours with nothing to do . . . I was staring at the trees in a nice quiet area and reflecting on how we could accelerate the process of self-discovery. Suddenly it came to me: why don't we take the age-old question of "Who am I?" which is at least seven thousand years old, and combine it with the communication methods I had learned? And that question "Who am I?" came together with the dyad format and thus was born the Enlightenment Intensive. It wasn't that I sat down and thought about it for a long time. I was just musing, "How is it that we could help people to accelerate this process of self-discovery?"*

He saw that he could have people sit in dyads just as he was already doing. They would take turns contemplating as in the ancient way, but also expressing to each other on a regular basis what had come into their awareness.

Charles ran some initial experiments with a few students. One of these was a tall, young electronics engineer named Edward Riddle, known to his friends as Edrid. Twenty-seven years later, he recalled that period just before the first Enlightenment Intensive:

> At that time we would spend Wednesday evenings working in dyads. During this period I noticed for the first time that some of the people were working on the question, "Who am I?" I was surprised at what they were going through while they were doing this. They had emotions coming up, and phenomena, liking shaking. Then, not long after this, I was with two or three people talking with them, and Charles came in. He said he had scheduled something completely new that could be really powerful. He said it would be called an "Enlightenment Intensive," and I said, "I'll do it!"

It was scheduled for the Fourth of July holiday weekend, over five days (the standard Enlightenment Intensive has long since been adjusted to three days). Following the uncompromising standards of the Zen patriarchs, Charles designed everything into the event to contribute to that purpose only. No drugs would be allowed, not even coffee or cigarettes. Meals would be light and vegetarian. There would be no opportunity for activities such as reading, going to restaurants, or watching TV. Most significant, no other meditation or growth processes would be mixed in with the pure practice of contemplating a key question and communicating to a listening partner in a dyad.

OUT TO THE DESERT

He decided to hold the trial run out on a piece of land the center had just purchased about sixty miles east of Los Angeles. The place was out where the Mojave Desert rises up into the foothills of the San Bernardino mountains, in a region known as Lucerne Valley. The country in these parts is high desert, sitting at elevations of several thousand feet or more. It's a dry and sandy place, home to lizards, horned toads, and rattlesnakes. There's a great wide sky above and long views to mountaintops in the distance. Lucerne Valley is not as hot and dry as the low deserts, but it's desert enough so that full-sized trees can't live there. The shrub-like flora that can be seen have names like greasewood, tumbleweed, and Spanish bayonet.

In the hours before the start of this first experiment, twenty-six people rolled up the dusty dirt road in their cars, ready to try whatever this thing was. They found the facilities not luxurious.

Edrid:

I remember on that first Enlightenment Intensive out in Lucerne Valley the physical conditions were pretty primitive. The place wasn't built up yet. We did the Intensive in a temporary structure built against the side of an old house trailer that was already there. It was made of a wood frame with plywood on top, all screened in. There were rugs on the ground, and we sat in the dyads on metal folding chairs. We didn't really know what we were in for, but I remember we just really went for it.

With Ava assisting and a couple of cooks to provide meals, Charles began the experiment. He explained that they were to try as best they could to continually ask themselves one of a few key questions: "Who am I?" "What am I?" "What is my true nature?" and "What is the purpose of life?" (These were eventually modified over the years to "Who am I?" "What am I?" "What is life?" and "What is another?") They were to seek to experience the actuality of their self or life rather

Contemplation in a Dyad

8

than just think about it intellectually or philosophically. They were to work as steadily at this as they could. His students already knew the basic dyad format, and this was an advantage. He told them that the schedule would run from early in the morning to nearly midnight, and that they would be spending a lot of time in dyads.

After the opening lecture, everyone chose a partner and sat down. Charles had them begin the process by finding out each other's contemplation question. Then he had one partner give the other the simple instruction, "Tell me who you are." (Or, according to what question was being worked on, "Tell me what you are," "Tell me your true nature," or "Tell me the purpose of life.")

REDISCOVERY OF THE STAGES TO ENLIGHTENMENT

Within the dyad periods, people took turns being the listening partner while the other person contemplated and communicated whatever came up. Each dyad period was followed by a break, a meal, a walk, or a lecture. There were also work periods, sitting contemplations, and an afternoon rest. Charles instructed people to "Hold your question," even during these times outside the dyads. He meant by this that they should continue to undistractedly ask themselves their question, seeking to resolve it by direct, experiential breakthrough. It was a very structured environment, yet there was great freedom in it for people to contemplate, express, process, and go through what they had to go through to encounter their own true nature. As the hours went by, various stages became observable. These did not appear in step-by-step order for everyone. But they appeared as common stages many people experienced as they worked on their question hour after hour.

ANSWERS

At first, answers and descriptions began coming up for most people. They began to say things to their partner such as: "Well, what I am is an architect, that's what I do, that's what I am" or, "Who I am is just me, that's pretty much it."

There was obviously some truth to these answers, but the mere answers didn't change anything.

INTELLECTUALISM AND LOGIC

People began to look more deeply, some turning to their education or logic for the solution: "Well, Nietzsche said that God is dead . . . " or: "Let's see, I'm looking out at you from in here, so I must be some kind of an entity existing behind my eyeballs somehow . . . "

These approaches seemed to go deeper, but they did not produce a fundamental change of consciousness.

MEMORIES

For most, sooner or later, memories began to come up, of childhood, old lovers, happy times or sad. "I'm remembering how my mother used to stand in the kitchen, near the stove, I have this image of her there . . . "

None of this was enlightenment, but it was useful to communicate all that came up as it occurred. And to whatever was said, no matter how brilliant or banal or tragic or historic, the listening partner would listen non-judgmentally and simply say, "Thank you," in acknowledgment.

This way of listening, of not trying to change or evaluate what the contemplator said, had the helpful effect of giving people the freedom to say whatever came up for them. People began to realize that they didn't have to perform in a certain way, as in school or at work. They didn't have to be a proper social being, or an improper one either. None of that mattered here. They could communicate what came up, whatever it was, as long as it didn't interfere with their partner. People began to like this kind of truth-walking, this being together in nonabusive honesty hour after hour, all of it leading to who knows where.

Communication in a dyad

INSIGHTS AND RELEASES

As the hours went by, as people began to encounter their inner restraints and fears, some of them began experiencing insights. They began to spontaneously have new realizations about their own life and neurotic patterns. Sometimes these came quietly, sometimes with deep emotional releases: "Oh God, I've just been trying to live for my parents! When do I get to live for me?" Or: "You know, I think I talk too much. I think I talk to avoid feeling what's really going on inside of me."

These had real therapeutic value. Whole layers of mental and emotional tension began to fall away. Some people began to appear lighter, more emotionally released, more in their bodies. But this was nothing different from what people were able to achieve in private sessions or in ordinary growth groups. Insights and releases were valuable, but they were not enlightenment.

TRYING TO SEE THE TRUTH

Sooner or later, most people began trying to see the truth. In an effort to locate the actuality of oneself, life or another, we tend to *look*, either into the inner space of the mind or outwardly. It's natural. When we are on a search for something in life we normally go looking: "Where am I? Ah! I'm behind my eyeballs! Okay, I'll go look there. Nope, I'm not there anymore, now I'm the one looking at the space behind my eyeballs. I am the looker! I need to somehow jump into the me that's looking."

Nowadays, the staff of an Enlightenment Intensive will call this stage "chasing." It is an inner search to locate the source of oneself at an experiential level.

NO-MAN'S LAND

Eventually, some people began to reach an unusual place of nothingness, where no thoughts were happening in the mind and nothing seemed important. A person would contemplate and . . . nothing would come up: "I can't believe it, there's nothing happening in my mind. I'm sitting here, aware . . . but I contemplate and nothing comes up. I'm just looking into empty space."

Was this enlightenment? Was this the famous void discussed in the Zen literature? Charles didn't think so. "Stay with it," he said. "Give up trying to see yourself. Just keep trying to directly experience *the one who is conscious of the nothing!*"

PHENOMENA

On through the second day they went. Some began to experience phenomena such as heat in the body or mild visual distortions. It was tempting to try to alleviate these kinds of occurrences or see them as some reason to stop the process. But they are well-known in Zen practice as something to ignore. For hundreds of years, Zen students have been excitedly bringing such experiences to their master, only to be told: "*Who* is feeling the heat! *Who* is the seer of the distortions! Go only for that! Who are *you?!*"

EMOTIONS

People were not going through these stages in regimental order, there was great variety and flow in what people were experiencing. Later, as they kept at it, there came periods when the room was filled with emotion. Some people were laughing, some sobbing, some contemplating deeply, some sitting in abject apathy. What was happening here?

Edrid:

I remember on the second day being fascinated and even startled by the general intensity of it all. I'd done growth processes before, but I'd never seen anything like this. I was seeing people working on their question and physically shaking from it, or crying out, or just sitting there staring at nothing. I started to think I was in some kind of madhouse. We know a lot about Enlightenment Intensives now, but then it was all completely new, and so unenvisioned.

SERENITY

Later, some people began going into profound states of serenity, experiencing a trouble-free inner peace they had never known: "I feel such an inner stillness. I just feel at peace with everything. I could stay here forever." Was *this* enlightenment? It was so attractive, so wonderful, that the temptation was strong to quit contemplating and just sit in it. But for centuries Zen masters have called this phase "the cave of Satan" or "the pit of pseudo-emancipation." It is a state so comfortable that, like a drug, it can lull the contemplator into complacency or, worse, into thinking the goal has been achieved.

CRISIS AND EGO-DEATH

Having reached the third day now, some fell into despair or acute fear of a new kind. These crises involved a kind of battle between what the ego wants and how things actually are. For example, the ego may want to make enlightenment happen, but it can't. Many an ego goes to its dying breath kicking and screaming in despair over this point. This crisis may also be associated with some core existential issue: "If I go any further, I'll die, or go crazy, or be annihilated, or be abandoned!" These crises, brought on by the natural process itself, tested people's interest in the truth and seemed to offer a choice point: do you really want the truth, or do you want to back off?

Although the group was an increasingly cohesive one, each person was going through the stages via his or her own unique process—some flowing, some lurching, some grinding to a halt, some taking great intuitive leaps, some carefully shaving away at their question in little paper-thin slices. The room became a cauldron of people in high states, low states, and everything in between. Some felt good and some bad. Some were throwing their head back and roaring like the Day of Judgment. Yet there was a direction to the apparent madness. The inner traveling was contained and directed, as each person returned again and again to his or her question.

ENLIGHTENMENT

Eventually inside this cauldron breakthroughs of a whole new kind began to occur. A young woman named Lila Rich was one of the first to experience a fundamental resolution to her question. In 1996 she looked back on that weekend:

In those days, I guess because of our youth and all the things that were going on then, we were really daredevilish to explore the unknown, to inquire into the mind and ourselves. I was actually a very shy person then. I think on my own I wouldn't have found many opportunities to learn much about myself or others. But on the Enlightenment Intensive I really had the opportunity to do that.

I was working on "Who am I?" I had been experiencing the process as sometimes fun and exciting and other times irritating, because of the long schedule and having to apply myself to the question. Sometime around the third day, after going through a lot of changes up to that point, I suddenly had an experience of who I am. At first, I didn't say anything to my partner. I was kind of sheepish.

But I had really experienced something and so I went up for an interview with Charles. I told him that 'I am me.' But it wasn't the words that were important. What was important was that this answer was coming from the me that I actually experienced, without alteration or fabrication. I felt like I was showing myself for the first time. The experience was not dramatic, it had a very soft but very genuine feeling to it.

Being able to express this to others made a complete difference for me. I felt like I was coming out with myself for the first time ever. I was really happy and I had a lot to say in the dyads after that. I had found some basic genuineness that allowed for real confidence. I really value that experience as finding the starting point to who I really am."

Others began to shatter the bottom of their question. Karen Lloreda, the mayor of a mid-sized city in California when I spoke with her in 1995, also directly experienced into her true nature:

We all went to that first Intensive with a lot of anticipation. However, I didn't have any idea as to what enlightenment was supposed to mean. I had the words but not any firsthand knowledge. But late in the Intensive I experienced a degree of enlightenment that has held strong for me since. What I experienced was extremely simple. I experienced that I am. I experienced that I am and always will be. There was no context to it, and I couldn't make any other assumptions. I just kept experiencing that I am, and always will be.

Whenever someone broke through, he or she spoke from a place so essential that the inner light of the pure individual came forth into the room as if from another world. These first few people began to communicate with an inner authenticity that had both depth and lightness, magically mixed together and based in their own direct experience of reality. Like Yon Kane's experience on the last day, the breakthroughs were sometimes explosive. For others they were softer, yet they arose from the same place of spontaneous union. By the end, around eight of the people had had such a breakthrough, and the enthusiasm for the event was high. Most of those who hadn't broken through into direct experience nonetheless felt clearer in themselves, having gained useful insights to bring into their life as well as having laid a foundation for further enlightenment work. The surprising workability of the approach had been confirmed: when continual contemplation of a key question was combined with repeated communication and understanding, the power of the two worlds came together in a new way. A synergy was generated that boosted the truth-walker's journey to self-realization.

Edrid:

When the breakthroughs started coming, they were beautiful. For a lot of us there, we could feel the significance of it all while it was happening. It was like we were ushering in some kind of new path, some kind of whole new way. Years later, as I saw Enlightenment Intensives take off and reach thousands of people around the world, I felt fortunate to have been a part of its beginning.

Charles was also surprised:

Son of a gun, if people didn't start having some direct experiences. I had expected it would take several Enlightenment Intensives for some enlightenments to start showing up. But to my amazement, people were having these experiences and it blew me out as much as it did them.

Drew Renner, now a corporate marketing specialist, was also impressed. In 1995, he remembered:

That first Enlightenment Intensive was a glorious experiment. We had a real pioneering spirit. I didn't have an enlightenment experience myself, but the whole process of all the dyads was transformative. I think it is really necessary for the Western mind to contemplate, but we are such an undisciplined people at that sort of thing. The Enlightenment Intensive structure provides that discipline, but it is more of a fun type of discipline, because you do it together with others. All the contact and communication really gets Westerners to stick at it.

This was the birth of the Enlightenment Intensive. Following that first experiment, Charles went on to further develop the method, making changes here and there as he understood more about how the whole process worked. He retired from giving them in 1976, after they were well established. In the passage of time the property in Lucerne Valley was sold and the center was closed. But a training course had been developed, and others carried on giving Enlightenment Intensives independently, in their own varying styles, some of them going on to train others. Throughout the 1970s and '80s, Enlightenment Intensives became established around the United States, Canada and Europe, as well as in a growing number of other countries. A powerful two-week format emerged in the late 1980s. Since that first weekend out in the desert, a lot has been tried with the method, a lot has been experienced, and a lot has been learned. It will take a number of chapters here to give a fuller report. The starting point to it all is our inner desire to know who and what we are, what life is, and what others really are.

ENLIGHTENMENT
AND THE SEARCH FOR TRUTH

THE ENLIGHTENMENT INTENSIVE WAS BORN of something native to who we are: our interest in the truth. The wanting to know what's real and what's true is a powerful, natural force within us that expresses itself in many forms. In high schools, for example, there is one kind of search for truth taking place in science class when students dissect a frog. Down the hallway, in the girl's lavatory, there may be a very different kind going on: *Do you think he likes me? Do you? What did he say?*

Any court system is meant to be a search for the facts in a case, so that justice may be served. The military invests a lot of effort into searching for the truth of the enemy's capabilities and intentions. Parents instinctually look for the truth of how their children can be protected. The list could go on and on. The truth about things opens the door to reality, survival, power, wisdom, and fulfillment. Having an interest in the truth is not something we have to add to ourselves; it's part of our nature, part of what we are about as humans. We are all truth-seekers.

THE SEARCH FOR TRUTH ITSELF

Of all the different kinds of searchings for truth that there are, there is one particular kind that begins when we take up the essential questions of our existence. This could be called not just the search for truth but the search for truth itself. This is the search for the truth of the truth, that ultimate, underlying place from which all relative truths come. Sometimes it's called the search for enlightenment, or for God, although those words may not be used at first, only later. It may be that a person is just lying in bed one night and starts to wonder, "Who am I really? What is this life I am in? Where did this reality come from?" Whatever the source of it may be, this inner questioning is the subtle aspect that has motivated men and women throughout the ages to try to penetrate the ultimate nature of reality and the self.

THE UNIVERSAL QUESTIONS

There are a few essential questions that people around the world, throughout history, and across cultures, have consistently taken up and grappled with when their interest in the ultimate realities arises. These are:

1) Who am I? This is a natural starting point. Success with this question, whether gradual or sudden, clarifies at a pure experiential level who is doing the seeking. This is a necessary ingredient for going into the deeper and more demanding stages of enlightenment and spiritual growth, as well as for simply living one's life more authentically. Resolution of the "Who am I?" question settles the starting point, the point of origin, for all that follows.

2) What am I? Many derivations of this exist, such as "What is my true nature?" The famous Zen *koan* "What was my face before my parents were born?" is another.

People sometimes wonder what the difference is between "who" and "what." The "Who am I?" question is like being a tree in a forest and asking oneself, "Which tree am I? There are all these trees around, but who am I?" The "What am I?" question is like asking, "What is a tree? I know who I am now, I know I am this tree and not the other trees, but what is the ultimate nature of a tree? Is it physical or nonphysical, or some combination? Or something else altogether? *What* am I?"

Historically, these questions have been used with different orientations in different systems. In India, for example, there are some old traditions of using the

"Who am I?" question exclusively as a meditation practice over a period of decades. There, the interpretation of "Who am I?" is that it is all-encompassing and includes all aspects of our true nature, indeed of everything, including God. Other traditions, such as Zen (and the Enlightenment Intensive), have used the question in its more limited form, seeing it as an important first stage of work to start with. In these systems, once one has directly experienced who it is that is contemplating, other questions are used, such as "What am I?" and it's variations.

With *koan* work, one could technically use any question and eventually reach some level of enlightenment. We could use "Why is there air?" or "What's the difference?" Some of the Zen *koans* indeed get pretty far-out. A famous and much-used one is "Mu!" which has no real meaning. These are all tools to break the contemplator out of his or her mind and into the condition of enlightenment, a state transcendent of language, the intellect, and every part of the mind. But the universal questions are unique in that they are more natural *koans*, arising from within the heart and mind and soul of seekers everywhere. They reflect our orientation and natural interest at the start of our search and help keep us facing into the essence of reality.

3) What is life? Or "What is the purpose of life?" Variations of this include "What is death?" Buddha himself, according to the stories, was originally motivated in his seeking by an inner passion to resolve the mystery of human suffering and discover the true nature of life and death.

4) What is God? This is certainly an ultimate question that, in its many forms, has arisen naturally around the world. The problem with this question is that, while universal and all-encompassing, it tends to exclusively engage the mind when most people go to contemplate it over an intensive three-day period. For enlightenment work in the context of Enlightenment Intensives, the question *"What is another?"* is used because it aims the contemplator at the actuality of another individual. A real other is much less of an abstraction for most people than is the ungraspable idea of God. With "What is another?" one sets out from the self, encounters whatever it is we call life, and contemplates an actual other, in an all-encompassing package. The dyad format, with the partner sitting right there, offers a unique opportunity for delving into this particular question. It is a more powerful and experientially rich question than is usually realized at first, which many of the personal accounts ahead show. It may well be a modern breakthrough in *koan* science.

These questions, and their many variations, being at the core of life and beyond, are challenging, especially when you take into account that the real enquiry begins only *after* the intellect has been chewed through. If taken to their ends by pure experience, they lead to deeper and more complete levels of enlightenment. The Enlightenment Intensive was designed to help people leave behind the endless trails of books, words, and ideas and begin this process in a real way, working on either "Who am I?," "What am I?," "What is life?" or "What is another?"

But what is enlightenment really? What is this "thing" that holy men and women throughout the ages have been talking about or not talking about?

ENLIGHTENMENT

Like all of life's extreme experiences it's ultimately indescribable. But one definition of enlightenment is that it is the direct experience of the true nature of the way things actually are. By "direct" is meant not merely "close" but literally "at one with." This state of union, and the awakened consciousness that pours forth from it, does not have to be called 'enlightenment'. Historically it has been given many names, as seekers in other times and cultures have experienced it and tried to articulate it in their own language. In Yoga it is called *anubhava*, or one of a number of other Sanskrit words that describe its different levels. In Zen it is called *kensho* or *satori*. In Taoism, *wu-wei*. Writings that have come down to us throughout recorded history from around the world give heavy weight to the notion that the state of enlightenment is inherent to our true nature as individuals and is not something to which any person, method, or religion may legitimately lay exclusive claim.

I use the terms 'enlightenment' and 'direct experience', and I use them interchangeably, only because I have grown used to them. Anyone could make up a new name or even say nothing about it. Still, by whatever name it is known, or even if by no name at all, enlightenment is not a fake, imagined, or superstitious thing. It is the direct experience of the ultimate reality. As the accounts in this book show, this experience fundamentally evolves the consciousness of individuals. Here is one brief example from an Enlightenment Intensive:

> I suddenly became conscious that my mind was way off to the side. It still existed, but it was at a distance. And in an instant I experienced that there is no separation. That I'm not separate from life . . . none of us are . . . there is a union there that is simply there. All our apparent separation is happening in the space of this eternal union. It's like there's this continual song going on, singing out the union and the praise of God, all the time.

The actual state of enlightenment is not a derivative experience, like hearing about the Grand Canyon from someone else or reading about how good an apple tastes. It is also not even an *experienced* experience, such as being fully present down in the Grand Canyon itself or biting into an actual apple. Enlightenment is something beyond a full experience through the senses and this is what makes it unusual and very difficult to put into words, and why it is sometimes confused with other kinds of heightened experiences. The direct union that is enlightenment does not subjectively imply something greater beyond itself. It is not symbolic of anything. It is the absolute reality itself.

There are many levels of enlightenment that one can experience and from which one can cultivate living. In the beginning these are shallower experiences, but no less real. In trying to explain the fact of these levels, a Zen master once said, "There are degrees of *kensho*. It is like two farmers looking at a man who is approaching them. One farmer is standing closer to the approaching man. The other farmer is standing more at a distance. The distant one says, "Someone is coming! But I can't tell who it is." The nearer one says, with clear certainty, "It's Yasuo, our neighbor! And he is bringing some apples!"

Thus, one can have a pure "Who am I?' enlightenment but still not know the fuller dimensions of one's "whatness," or true nature. One may not know the nature of life, but the simple issue of "Who am I?" may be settled at the core. The levels of enlightenment include increasing depths of realizations of the totality of all being, nonbeing, and the nature of absolute reality. The many direct experiences described in this book show some of these different levels.

It happens sometimes that individuals have enlightenment experiences in the normal course of life. This includes young people. I have a friend who, as a teenager, was lying on her bed one afternoon listening to a Beatles song. She happened to be in love at the time and was just lying there idly thinking, in a more-than-usual state of openness. Suddenly she directly experienced who she is. She had no language at the time to speak about the experience, but years later she took up Zen practice and Enlightenment Intensives, finding in them a natural context for going deeper with what she had experienced.

Extreme circumstances can also sometimes bring about direct experience. I met a man in Europe once who told me he had directly experienced his true nature while being tortured by the KGB during World War II. His description had the ring of authenticity and he spent the remainder of his life approaching every relationship with a sacred orientation. An Israeli friend of mine told me he had an enlightenment experience while on the receiving end of an Egyptian artillery barrage in the Sinai during the Yom Kippur War. He spent the next three days in a state of ecstasy and oneness, riding in an armored vehicle at night and fighting during the day. Previously an aimless teenager whose sole interest was sex, his life after that became a spiritual quest to deepen and integrate what he had experienced.

However, as popular methods for self-awakening, the tactics of the KGB and Egyptian artillery units never really caught on. Although such random breakthroughs are possible in life just by happenstance, many for whom this has not happened look for somewhere to go to enhance the possibility that it will.

WHERE TO GO FOR ENLIGHTENMENT?

Here there is a problem. The Yellow Pages are not usually a big help. Universities, if the subject is dealt with at all, are committed to theoretical and literary approaches. For personal reasons a lot of people become disappointed with the religion of their youth. Books on enlightenment (like this one) can serve as pointers but are no substitute for real practice. The general lack of enlightenment tradition here in the West has thus driven many seekers to the East, or to Eastern teachings brought to the West. This approach has a lot of built-in challenges because of all the problems of language, culture, and tradition that come with the clashing of two worlds. Thus, a lot of people who have been drawn to the teachings of the East have had to somehow resolve how to integrate Eastern teachings and practices into their Western mind and brain and lifestyle. Among Westerners interested in enlightenment, in fact, the last part of this century has been a time of a lot of experimentation and discovery on this subject. In this process some individuals have succeeded in using Eastern methods for enlightenment. There are more and more Westerners now who have genuinely matured in their explorations into Eastern methods and are coming into their own as legitimate teachers of enlightenment. But no single Eastern method, in its pure form, has been widely embraced here in the West.

Instead, over the last four decades, one can see that we Westerners have been not only exploring Eastern influences but also trying to establish a working tradition of enlightenment we can call our own. A lot of books on enlightenment written by Western authors now share library shelves with ancient teachings from the East. In the 1970s, a seminar-style genre for beginning stages of enlightenment even appeared in America. These now come in lots of variations, combining approaches from the East with approaches from the West.

The Enlightenment Intensive, not being a religious system, and not being run seminar-style but rather dyad-style, is a well constructed place in our culture now where people can work solely on their own enlightenment and have practical guidance at every step. This method was born in the West and is highly suitable to the Western temperament. Generally, the Enlightenment Intensive is a little more challenging than seminar-style groups because it calls upon people to work at their question in a self-responsible way, face-to-face with another person, as opposed to sitting theater-style in a large group. On the other hand, a wide variety of people young and old may easily participate. And the method permits working into deeper levels of awakening, according to one's interest.

TRANSFORMATION AND THE BENEFITS OF ENLIGHTENMENT

The transformative power of a genuine enlightenment experience that has some depth to it, under whatever circumstances it might occur, is without a doubt one of the most impressive experiences a person can have in life. Yet in practical terms the results can be quite unexpected. I remember a woman who by her own report had a two-year-old son who cried most of the time, no matter what she tried. Crying and whining were his basic mode of being in life. Then one weekend she went to an

Enlightenment Intensive and directly experienced who she is. When she went home and began relating to her son, she found she could contact him on a more real basis. To her surprise, he stopped crying and whining so much. After this he would cry only when there was something obvious to cry about. She told me she felt that something in her basic relationship with him had been resolved just by the increase in her own experience of her true self and by her ability to relate to him authentically. Something vital that the baby had been missing was now there: his mother relating from who she really is, contacting him as he really is.

We all suffer when our experience of relating is that, "Others don't see *me*." How much pain and neurosis in the world is based on this single flaw in relating: when we don't truly see who we each are?

One of the greatest contributions that the Enlightenment Intensive makes on a social basis is the evolution of this capacity. But what happens outwardly for an individual can vary widely. Sometimes after an enlightenment experience a person may make major life changes, letting go of an unsatisfactory career, relationship, or approach to life, and moving on to another career, relationship, or approach. This is especially true if the person had built a life based on a false personality or a system of "shoulds" and "shouldn'ts" that had nothing to do with who he or she actually is.

Sometimes a person will make no outward changes at all, there will only be a subtle shift in being more present in the life and relationships that are there. In this sense, seeking enlightenment involves some risk, because there are no guarantees what the outcome will be. It is not possible to predict what movement will take place in a person's growth process once he or she has experienced a whole new infusion of reality. It is possible to predict that the direction is likely to be towards more truth and authenticity, whatever form that might take.

How people describe the benefits of enlightenment varies widely but has some recurring themes. There are common statements like, "I experienced who I really am" or, "I came home to myself for the first time." In the early stages a person might express something like this with great enthusiasm. Years later, it might be quietly stated as a simple fact of what happened. People who continue into enlightenment work tend to discover others more deeply than before. Relationships and spirituality become richer, with more dimensions, more reality. Many people experience that with enlightenment, some part of their inner search has ended forever. The essential pathway to fulfillment has opened up. The task now is to walk that path, to live it, rather than to simply seek. There is no price that one can put on these benefits. In the chapters ahead are more detailed descriptions of how these benefits have affected the lives of individuals with different backgrounds and interests.

With enlightenment, it is not necessary to have a clear concept of the thing or to "understand" it before setting out for it. We don't need a clear idea of what the truth is before intending to know it. The intending to know is sufficient to begin with. And when we are ready to take up this search into the essential questions of our existence, we need a laboratory in which to work. One we now have is the Enlightenment Intensive. There, most people begin by working on the age-old question, "Who am I?"

WHO AM I?
BREAKTHROUGH ON AN ANCIENT QUESTION

WHAT IS IT LIKE TO ACTUALLY TAKE a a three-day Enlightenment Intensive and work toward self-enlightenment, eventually breaking through? Each person's experience is unique, and indeed, most will not be successful in their first try. Here is an account of a young American woman who took her first Enlightenment Intensive in 1979 and was fortunate to have an enlightenment experience on her first attempt. She was twenty-seven when she spoke with me in 1982.

JAYNE

I first heard of Enlightenment Intensives about two years before I took one. But when I saw the brochure, all I read is that you sit across from someone for three days and you talk about who you are. And it just sounded so scary and so horrible that I thought I could never do it. In those days, I felt really alienated from people and found them hard to get close to. So I just filed the brochure away.

For many, there is some real apprehension about the prospect of taking an Enlightenment Intensive. It is not a usual type of activity. It is often not clear at first that there are many support systems built into the method, or that people go forward at their own rate. However, when someone first hears of the Enlightenment Intensive, a seed is planted, and this seed may later sprout into an inner call to do one.

A SPROUTING OF INTEREST

Then, as time went on, with my job and everything that I was involved with, things seemed like they were okay but the trouble was that I felt like this disconnected thing over here that wasn't quite sure where it fit in. So things still weren't right. Then one day I was cleaning out my bookshelves and the Enlightenment Intensive brochure fell out. And it had written on it, "Tell me who are you." And I thought, "That's what I need to know! I need to know who I am! I haven't been showing up in my own life!"

This sense of somehow being separated from one's own life, even if one happens to be outwardly successful, is a hallmark of a life being lived from ideas, social automaticity, or an inner system of shoulds and shouldn'ts. It's a hallmark of a life not lived from who one really is.

So it became clear to me then that I wanted to do it, and I sent off for the information. Then I went to a Preview, and I liked the master who spoke there. So I took the next one.

THE MASTER

The people who run Enlightenment Intensives are called masters. This isn't to say that they are *addressed* as "master." If you want to speak to one you use his or her first name.

People are sometimes suspicious of this term "master," thinking it might mean you have to join a cult or take on a guru. You don't, but the word is not arbitrarily used. To guide and support someone into the state of direct experience takes a kind of knowledge, certainty, and personal involvement that are special to this field. The traditional Zen term "master" embodies these qualities and was thus carried over to the Enlightenment Intensive method.

A "Preview" is a public talk that some masters give periodically to explain what the Enlightenment Intensive is all about. It's natural to want to meet the person who will be giving the event to see if it feels right to go ahead.

LEARNING THE ROPES

When the Intensive began, I started working on the question, "Who am I?" And I remember that, both at the Preview and on the first morning, the master talked about how there were rules, like no smoking or gossiping or evaluating what people express as a result of their contemplation. He talked about how the Intensive was tightly scheduled and free from distractions. And he talked about how that might bother some people. But my immediate experience on the first day, which grew and became stronger, was that I was just so relieved that here was a place where things were taken care of to the last detail, so I could just concentrate on this question of who I really am.

The rules and structure are necessary boundaries within which people may begin to open up without fear of harmful evaluations from others or time-consuming distractions. (For a list of the rules of an Enlightenment Intensive, see Chapter 5.)

The first day I gradually got into the process and got more comfortable with the dyads and the people. Then, early on the second day, the first really powerful thing happened for me. Somebody down the row had a direct experience of who he is. Before that time, my mind was trying to figure out my problems and get this answer to who I am. And I had never done any previous spiritual practice or anything, so the whole idea of the 'truth' really didn't mean much to me. But when I saw this other person have a direct experience, all of a sudden I got a real sense that there was something else out there that was so much more than what I thought I was there for.

For many the first day and a half is a journey from the realm of ideas into the realm of reality. 'Truth' and 'enlightenment' may begin as concepts in the overmentalized world of the participant's mind, but with the regular practice of contemplation and truthful expressions a new focus, a new zeal, and a new sense of direction may emerge.

THE AWAKENING OF THE PASSION FOR TRUTH, AND FACING BARRIERS

So I kept working at my question and I began to go through a lot of stuff. These questions or doubts or fears would come up on walks or during a dyad. And I'd be afraid to go up and talk to the master or even any of the monitors about them. But the master would talk a little bit before each dyad or during the lecture, and he would zero right in on what was going on for me. He talked about the barriers that come up, the doubts and the fears, and all the things that were actually coming up for me. To me it was like, "Wow, these people know what I'm going through." So my unasked questions kept getting answered, and I began to do the contemplation technique really well.

The words of advice and encouragement from the master turn out to be essential to people's progress. We each have our own unique way of going through the process of the Enlightenment Intensive, but at the same time the basic kinds of barriers that come up and the ways to get through them are well known. They have actually been well known for thousands of years in other traditions, and they are well known now as they apply to this particular method. The body of practical knowledge that the master and staff possess (described in Chapters 5–14) is one of our best friends in this process.

Then, during the dyad before the walk on the third and final night, something happened. I had this really intense communication with my partner in the dyad. She really shared with me exactly what was going on for her, and it really moved me. I went out on the walk still really moved by this. And as I worked on my question, walking along and looking at the ground, I guess I was just more open than usual.

ENLIGHTENMENT

And what happened is that I looked up from the ground at one point and all of a sudden my consciousness shifted into a place where I experienced no separation from anything. I felt a connectedness with everything. And out of all that stuff, I experienced exactly who I am. I experienced the me that I am, that I always have been and always will be.

The enlightenment experience, which does not take place for every participant, is a spontaneous breakthrough occurring at some unexpected moment. Along with the direct experience itself, there are also often what are called phenomena. These are not in themselves the enlightenment experience; rather, they are the energy and

30

perceptual side-effects attendant to the core instant of union. These vary according to each person's particular mental, emotional, and physical makeup.

TRANSFORMATION AND IMMEDIATE SIDE-EFFECTS

And even though it was dark, everything took on this glow. I'd also been really tired the last couple of dyads before, but all of a sudden I had all this energy. And I kept walking around waiting for something to be wrong. But I was in this state of experiencing everything as it actually is. It was like someone had taken the world and turned it, like an eclipse. Something had been blocked and it wasn't blocked any more. And I started laughing out loud because at that moment it just seemed so absurd that I had spent these grueling days asking this question, "Who am I?" It just seemed so absurd that it had never occurred to me who I am! It wasn't like I came up with anything that was different about me. I was still me. My personality was still the same, my life was still the same, I was basically still the same person. But I had this experience that I'd never had before. And in it there was this total, incredible clarity of everything exactly as it is.

There is a basic shifting of consciousness and orientation within reality here, that is in a general way typical of enlightenment experiences. One can sense from Jayne's words that this transformation occurred spontaneously, at the core, rather than from a new set of ideas coming in from someone else or some other external source. Expressing this new condition sometimes makes the experiencer sound nonordinary, perhaps even mad. Statements like "I experienced the me that I am" or "Everything is as it really is" may sound truly banal by ordinary standards. But when they come from reality itself being directly experienced, they are expressions of inner transformation. Jayne would have been instructed by the master to continue communicating about the breakthrough to her partners, letting it flow out and settle into the cells of her body and her being. In a well-presented experience, it is also common that the person goes home and begins seeing life in new ways.

RETURN TO LIFE

After the Intensive I was just flying for about the next four days. I had a lot of energy and I felt that I was being myself and relating from myself for the first time in my life. It was really freeing. And it was something that had somehow gotten integrated into my being. As I would talk to people, I could see that it was really me I had experienced directly; it wasn't just something that had happened to me and was gone. It had this lasting effect that is still with me. I never again experienced that alienation I used to feel before. The alienation is just not there now.

This is significant; it wasn't just an enlightenment that Jayne experienced, it was *herself*. We call it an enlightenment experience after the fact, but in the experience itself there's more a sense that, "This isn't just an *experience*, it's *me!*" Jayne began presenting herself as she is, rather than merely recalling an experience that took place in the past.

Since then, in my friendships and relationships with people, I'm more open to who they are. I don't have so many preconceived notions about how this person needs to be as my friend, or whatever the relationship is. I'm more open to having them be who they are, getting to know them and letting them just teach me who they are, so I can experience them. And before, I used to talk to people all the time, but I wasn't really letting them know what was going on for me, so things always got weird. I can take the risk more now.

An enlightenment experience can also impact how a person afterwards views spirituality and growth. It can change forever how a person views the question of how to find truth in life:

The thing about Enlightenment Intensives is that the question "Who am I?" aims you at the real you, the real thing. And it's really there. I go to a university now, and it has an entire graduate program in Consciousness Studies. And I'm really glad that there are groups of people who are paying more attention to that element of life. But so much of it is talking about it and creating more ideas and writing books, and there is usually the same frustration of how to experience it, and how to bring it into life. And Enlightenment Intensives, rather than giving you another set of beliefs about how everything is or should be, they just sit you down so you can really do it. You can go through what you need to go through to do it, for yourself.

At the time, Jayne was someone with no previous meditation training, who had grown up in America doing the normal things Americans do. Yet in three days she had had a beginning level of enlightenment. In Zen monasteries her experience would be considered a clear *kensho* experience, an important inner cornerstone upon which to build a richer life and a deeper spiritual practice.

How can this happen? What are the inner workings of this unusual process, at first so strange-sounding for most people? An Enlightenment Intensive is not run seminar-style, is not like school or a church service, and is, in fact, unlike virtually every other environment a person is likely to have encountered in life. In the following chapters are transcriptions of lectures that give all the basic information, such as the rules and schedule and how to work on one of the questions. There are also interviews between the master and people working on their question. And there are further accounts of people breaking through into the mysterious land of direct experience.

ON AN ENLIGHTENMENT INTENSIVE: FIRST EVENING TALK

ORIENTATION,
WHICH QUESTION TO WORK ON,
AND STAFF INTRODUCTIONS

ENLIGHTENMENT INTENSIVES ARE GIVEN in different styles by different masters, but there is a basic structure and technique that are commonly followed in regard to the essential points. These are explained to people during the lectures, which come at times when participants most need to hear them. There is no doubt that these lectures have more impact when they are heard in context, at stages in the process when people are in a position to immediately apply what is learned. Here they will be useful to clarify practical aspects and give more of a flavor of the work.

The following lectures, shortened for use here, were cassette-recorded during an Enlightenment Intensive I gave in a large house in Oakland, California, May 12–15, 1988. There were twenty-four participants. A married couple had come in from Toronto. One woman had come in from Florida. An Englishman who had taken Enlightenment Intensives in England was also there. The rest were from around California. I remember that one was a graduate student from Stanford, another a computer engineer from the Silicon Valley area just south of San Francisco. One was a martial artist from Berkeley, one a therapist from Los Angeles. The makeup of the group was as varied as I'd come to expect.

The staff had arranged the large living room so that it was cleared of any big furniture; cushions and chairs were available. The master normally sits in a chair at one end, from which to easily watch over the whole room. He or she is like the captain of a ship bound for distant lands, and this first evening is when the final preparations are made for sailing away the next day. When everyone had arrived and completed their registration, the staff called the group together in the main room, and we began:

> In my opinion, what you are about to do is one of the most valuable ways you can spend three days of your life. It's three days for the truth of yourself, of life and of others. And afterwards you can do what you want with what you have experienced. Everything I'm going to be doing here will be to give you the best opportunity to break through into an enlightenment experience. To get to the place where there is a real possibility for that means getting over any process of thinking, believing, seeing, feeling, intuiting, being good, being bad, struggling forward, and so on. At some point along the way, your interest in the truth may be tested, not by me, but by the very nature of the undertaking. As you open up more deeply to what

is, as you begin to process through your normal view of reality, something in you may begin to protest. Things may get boring or weird or scary or almost anything else. But anything worth doing in life has some challenge to it, and a challenge is much easier to face when it's occurring in a basically supportive and uplifting process, which this is. You'll have a lot of support on your journey here from me and the staff. It's all we'll be doing for these three days. We'll be explaining things as we go and there will be lots of opportunities for you to come and talk with us about your process if you need to.

It's important that you have your own experience, rather than mine or someone else's. So, in these three days I'm not going to be telling you anything about who you are, what you are, what life is, or what another is. I won't be teaching a religion or saying anything about what I think the ultimate truth is. I won't be telling you how to live or how to deal with any life problems you might be experiencing. What I'll be doing is a lot of guiding and supporting you in what it takes to get through the barriers to you directly experiencing the actuality of yourself, life, or another. This is the purpose the Enlightenment Intensive was designed for, and it's what it does best at.

On the first day here there is a kind of decompression process that most people go through to some degree. You'll be disengaging from your normal life, from the usual busy-ness of it—the routines, the concerns you have, and all that. Your biological clock will be adjusting to the schedule, and the cells of your body will be getting used to going without coffee and cigarettes and TV and whatever your usual habits are. You'll also be learning the contemplation and communication technique that I'll explain later on. So there's usually a transition period at first for most people. And after a while you'll be through it.

CHOOSING A QUESTION

What question should you work on? Well, if it's your first time taking an Intensive, and you are under forty-five, start with "Who am I?" If it's your first Intensive and you have a strong pull to do "What am I?" come talk to me; that may also be an option you could go with. But check it with me first. If it's your first Intensive, you are over forty-five, and the question "What is life?" interests you more, go ahead and choose that.

If you've completed an Enlightenment Intensive before, whether or not you had a direct experience, go ahead and choose which question interests you the most, either "Who am I?" "What am I?" "What is life?" or "What is another?" Generally it's best to stay on a question until you break through to at least one level, but this is not always the case. Go ahead and talk to me about this if you are in doubt. Once you choose your question, stay with that one unless you talk to me first.

If you work on "Who am I?" or "What am I?", you'll be going for the truth of your self. If you start to think about that, it can get tricky. "Well, it's evident that I'm here, but who is it? What is it?" After you go through your ideas about it, it can start going around in circles and slip through your fingers. It can start to drive you nuts, because this is not about philosophy or teachings or coming up with the right answer so that you can get a good grade. It's not about acting socially appropriate. It's about contemplating on the actuality of your self with the intention to realize it directly. Most of us weren't trained much in school about how to deal with this kind of activity, but here you will be.

You may decide to work on "What is life?" What is all this around us and in us and between us that we call life? It is obvious that there is something going on. But what is it? If you keep putting your attention on that you'll tend to meet up with failure again and again, because it is not easy to resolve this question. This makes this work hard on the ego. Yet life keeps being whatever it is. And all it takes is one success in direct experience to make all those failures be worth it. That's why we keep at it.

You may choose to work on "What is another?" Others are obviously there, but what are they? Are they like me, or are they different? Okay, they're human. But what's a human?

In this technique you have a total support system for staying at your question, through all the failed attempts and through all the tricks and protests of the mind, the emotions and the body. This support takes many forms. You have a dyad partner, whom you'll change after each forty-minute period. You have myself and the staff. You have the schedule. You have this contemplation and communication technique which I'll be teaching you. It's called the Enlightenment Technique and it is a powerful tool for dealing with all the little and big things which are bound to come up as you go to work on your question.

We'll begin tomorrow morning. The monitors will wake you at six, and you'll have fifteen minutes to get dressed, use the toilet, and come to the main room. At that time I'll go over the schedule, the ground rules, and the Enlightenment Technique.

THE STAFF

I'll introduce the staff to you. Would you each just raise your hand when I introduce you?

THE SENIOR MONITOR

Thom is the Senior Monitor, which means he's experienced and knowledgeable about helping you with the Enlightenment Technique, which I'll be explaining tomorrow morning. You can always talk to him if you are having some difficulty about any aspect of this process, or if you just want to talk about what's happening for you. Any of the monitors may also sit near your dyads sometimes to see how you're doing.

THE CHIEF MONITOR

Glenn is the Chief Monitor. He's in charge of the physical environment and all logistics, making sure they run smoothly so you can forget about them and just work on your question. If you need an extra blanket or anything like that, speak to Glenn.

THE MONITOR

Hashim is a monitor, which means he'll be helping out with the environment and in the kitchen, and in the general running of things. You can talk with Hashim about what's going on for you, and he may also ask you how it's going sometimes.

THE DE-ODDER

Bret is a monitor, and also what's called the de-odder, which means he may sit in as a participant if we are an odd number instead of an even number. This is so everyone has a partner to work with in the dyads.

THE COOKS

Evelyn is the chief cook, and she'll be helped by Heidi and Jane. The food will be balanced vegetarian, and you'll get moderate portions of it so that your body will be supported but you won't be weighed down by having to digest a big meal.

This is really an adventure, what we're doing. Try to be open to it being that, it will help. Even though we won't leave this room much, we'll really be traveling. Your main job tonight is to just try to get some sleep. And go ahead and start thinking about your question if you want. You can get a running start this way.

After several practical questions, it was time for people to start bedding down. Twenty minutes later, when everyone was settled down, Glenn turned off the lights, and the house grew quiet. Tomorrow would be the beginning of three days for the truth.

5

FIRST DAY, MORNING LECTURE

THE RULES, SCHEDULE,
AND THE ENLIGHTENMENT TECHNIQUE

"GOOD MORNING." Glenn's voice quietly but solidly pierces the mists of sleep. "This is the first day of your Enlightenment Intensive. You have fifteen minutes to get up and get ready for the lecture."

As Glenn turns the lights up low, some people are already up and getting dressed, going to the toilet, and putting things away. Before long everyone has gathered in the main room in the quiet of the morning and the first light of the day outside. Most wear sleepy faces. In this talk, we have to go over all the basics:

In a direct experience, there is no process of experience or perception through the senses going on. The mind usually has a real hard time with that idea. Another way to say this is that we are going for a state of union between you and reality itself, in some measure. There is always some risk to this, because one is trying to experience into places beyond one's known experience. Even if you've had direct experiences before, the next level is unknown to you, and the same risks are there. You may think, "What if what I find is unacceptable? What if my boyfriend doesn't approve? What if I find out I'm something I don't want to be?"

These are the beginning considerations. I can't give you any absolute guarantees about how it's all going to turn out. But the fact that I am sitting here shows you that I think what you're about to undertake is worth it. And it is always best to start simply where you are at, and not try to be in some elevated place that you're not, or even to try to re-create a past high experience you may have had. This is a process of resorting to truth, and that includes the simple truth around you and within you, of simply starting where you're at. There is great relief in this approach, and it's the one I encourage you to take.

I'll explain the rules now, and the schedule, and then the Enlightenment Technique which we use here.

THE RULES

The rules are all here to support you in what you're trying to do. They are known by long experience to do this. The first is:

1. Use only the technique taught here.

There are a lot of other meditation techniques that are good, but you will dilute your efforts here by combining them. After the three days are over you are certainly free to continue with your usual practices, if you have one.

2. No judgments or laying trips on others.

"Trip laying" is a term which means to judge or invalidate someone or what he or she has said or experienced. If you say to your partner, "That was pretty sick, what you just communicated there," that's a trip. People tend to close down if they sense they will be evaluated or even spoken about, and we don't want that.

3. Set aside sexual activity.

Set it aside just for these three days. This includes masturbation. It's okay to communicate sexual thoughts or feelings if they occur as a result of your contemplation, but do so without involving or making references to your partner.

4. No gossiping

Gossip here means speaking about anything other than what's going on for you in your process. It's any talk that is off the purpose of what we are doing here.

5. Remove your jewelry, watch, and makeup, and plan to go without shaving, colognes, deodorants, and other scents.

You'll have time to shower and stay clean, but for these three days set aside the extras. You won't need a watch because the monitors will let you know when it's time to pick a partner for a dyad or take a walk, or whatever is next. This way, you will be free to work continually on your question without having to think about time or deal with the extras such as jewelry.

6. Eat only the food served.

You don't have to eat it all, but don't eat more. You'll have three light meals and two snacks, so you'll be all right food-wise.

7. Go ahead and go to the toilet at any time without permission, except during a lecture, sitting contemplation, and the start of any dyad; take no longer than necessary.

Just go do it and come back.

8. No smoking, drugs, alcohol, coffee, or caffeinated tea.

You may go through some withdrawal on the first day, but thousands of people have done it, so be encouraged. If you are taking a medication, talk to me about it at the break. Coffee drinkers in particular sometimes get a headache for a while as part of the detoxification process. This can be unpleasant, but it should pass after a while and then you'll be through it.

9. Follow the schedule.

The announcements of the staff will tell you what's next on the schedule.

10. Leave in your car or with a staff person all books, magazines, journals, radios, cellular phones, laptops, and anything else that might be a distraction to you.

Store them away, or if you think you will be sorely tempted, give them to one of the monitors to keep until the end.

That's it, those are the ground rules, and they will support you in what you are trying to do. Try to get into their spirit and make them your own.

THE SCHEDULE

At this point the schedule is outlined.

6:00–6:15 a.m.	Rise
6:15–7:00	Dyad
7:00–7:15	Physical Exercise
7:15–7:30	Herbal Tea Break
7:30–8:15	Dyad
8:15–8:45	Breakfast
8:45–9:30	Dyad
9:30–10:15	Dyad
10:15–11:15	Walking Contemplation
11:15–12:00 p.m.	Dyad
12:00–12:45	Lunch
12:45–1:30	Dyad
1:30–2:15	Lecture
2:15–2:45	Sitting Contemplation
2:45–3:30	Dyad
3:30–3:45	Snack
3:45–4:30	Dyad (sometimes a Working Contemplation)
4:30–5:30	Rest Period
5:30–6:15	Dyad
6:15–7:00	Dinner
7:00–7:45	Dyad
7:45–8:30	Dyad
8:30–9:30	Walking Contemplation
9:30–10:15	Dyad
10:15–10:45	Breathing Exercises and snack
10:45–11:30	Dyad
11:30	To bed

You'll be spending a lot of time in dyads, and working intensively. However, the schedule has a good balance in it and thousands of people young and old have gone through it, so be heartened.

THE FORTY-MINUTE DYAD AND THE ENLIGHTENMENT TECHNIQUE FOR CONTEMPLATING AND COMMUNICATING

After this lecture here there will be a short tea break, and then we'll have the first dyad. This is the main practice here. For a dyad, you pick a partner and sit down facing each other either on cushions or chairs. I'll have you find out from your partner what question he or she is working on. Then I'll have you begin.

1. Beginning the Dyad

You begin by having one partner, who I will indicate, give a specific instruction to the other. If your partner is working on "Who am I?" you'll say, "Tell me who you are." If your partner is working on "What am I?", give the instruction, "Tell me what you are."

If your partner is working on "What is life?" you say, "Tell me what life is." If your partner's question is on what another is, you say, "Tell me what another is."

Then your partner will have five minutes to contemplate and communicate what comes up. Then you change over. And you get your turn to contemplate and communicate for five minutes.

So structurally, the dyad format is very simple. It gives everyone equal time to contemplate and communicate. But, more specifically, how do you do this? Here we use a way called the Enlightenment Technique. When it is your turn to work in the dyad, this is what to try to do:

2. Receive the instruction

Suppose you are working on "Who am I?" Your partner will say, "Tell me who you are." What you do first is to receive the instruction. Don't ignore it or somehow hold it out. Let it in. Take it as a real communication from your partner.

3. Get a sense of yourself in the moment

Then you contemplate. To do this, first get a sense of yourself in the moment, just your ordinary sense of yourself now. You might get a sense of, "Well, I'm just sitting here looking at my partner." Fine. Start with whatever is obvious.

4. Intend to directly experience yourself

Then set out or intend to directly experience that self that you get a sense of, which is to say, you. Do the best you can at that. Basically, just go for the truth of you, directly. You might repeat the question to yourself, and that's all right, but do so with intention to know the truth of you directly. This is different from mindless repetition of the question.

5. Be open to whatever occurs

Then be open to whatever comes up, in your mind, your feelings, or your body. Don't try to make things be some way, or be in some past experience that you've had or heard about somewhere. Just be as open as you can to whatever is occurring as a result of your intending to experience yourself directly.

6. Communicate it to your partner

Then take whatever it was that occurred and communicate it to your partner, not leaving anything out or adding anything.

Then repeat the process until the five-minute gong sounds. The monitor will announce, "Thank your partner, change over."

7. Acknowledgment

At this point your partner should say, "Thank you." Then you give the instruction "Tell me who you are" (or the appropriate one) to your partner, so he or she gets a turn while you listen.

That's it. This dyad goes for forty minutes, so you each have four turns to contemplate and communicate, and four turns to listen. It's a good balance that works.

8. Stay with your question

When you are not in a dyad, stay with your question as much as you can. Work on the contemplation steps, and when you are next in a dyad you can communicate what occurred. In this way, spend as much of the time as you can going for the truth of what you are trying to directly experience. The breaks are mainly for your body, they aren't for you to back off on the technique.

Thus are the basics explained. Now, after a short tea break, the real process begins.

THE ENLIGHTENMENT TECHNIQUE:

Her partner says, "Tell me who you are."

She contemplates the question, "Who am I?"...

...and then communicates to her partner what occurred.

She will continue to contemplate and communicate for five minutes, when a gong will sound. At that point her partner will say "Thank you" and the roles will reverse. Thus, over the forty minute dyad period, each will have equal turns.

GETTING TO IT

Everyone picks a partner and sits down in a dyad. And with this the sails come down, the ship points its bow to the horizon, and it slips out of the harbor. A ripple of voices move up and down the row as the various instructions are given. Before long, the contemplating partners begin communicating the things that have come up as a result of contemplating. In the beginning, what people have to say is often very ordinary:

> *"God, I had a terrible night. I slept about four hours. I had this dream but I don't remember it."*

> *"I keep thinking about something my husband said to me before I came here. We sort of had this fight, and it's just kind of stuck here in my mind. I don't know what we're going to do about each other."*

> *"Well, I feel pretty good this morning. Who I am is feeling pretty good."*

Newcomers are sometimes shy at this stage and speak quietly or not much at all as they slowly relax into this unusual situation. Gradually, people lose their self-consciousness and begin to communicate more naturally to their partners.

INTERVIEWS

Throughout the day, people will sometimes come up to the master with questions about the technique. These brief interviews are important for giving technical guidance as well as contact and encouragement. The master must know how to deal with a wide variety of problems, questions, and experiences, and keep people on track to enlightenment as opposed to other kinds of experiences.

FIRST DAY INTERVIEWS
WITH THE MASTER

GETTING ON TRACK

THERE ARE SO MANY WRONG WAYS to go in this work, and the tricks of the mind so numerous and subtle, that the contact and practical guidance from someone who is experienced is vital. Theoretically, interviews are not necessary, since all of the essential information is given in the lectures. But in practice, when the bitter guerrilla war waged by the mind is in full swing, they are usually necessary.

These interviews were not recorded, in order to avoid the possible inhibiting effects on the participant. They were written down afterwards, some by me, some by other masters. Interviews may sometimes be lighthearted and even funny, but they are kept purposeful by the master. There is no tradition with Enlightenment Intensives that you bow down or do any ritual in the interview. You simply go up to where the master is sitting and sit on a nearby stool or chair. The following interviews are representative of some of the common issues that come up for people during the first day.

INTERVIEW 1:
SHYNESS TO COMMUNICATE

Master: *"This is your first Intensive, isn't it?"*

Linda, aged forty-one: *"Yes."*

"How's it going so far?"

"Well, I'm still not very comfortable in the dyads, especially with communicating to strangers. I don't know what to do about that. I feel shy, and I'm not sure what to communicate."

"Well, some shyness is completely normal here at first. It's a new environment for you. Are you communicating to your partner that you're shy?"

"No."

"Well, go ahead and communicate that, it's what's coming up for you."

"I thought I was supposed to say other things."

"Well, you're meant to say what's occurring for you when you contemplate, whatever it is. You're feeling shy. That's the simple truth. Go ahead and start right there, it's okay."

"Okay, I'll try."

INTERVIEW 2:
THE ERROR OF TRYING TO RECREATE
A PREVIOUS EXPERIENCE

Master: *"How's it going now?"*

Lisa, aged thirty-one: *"Well, I'm having some trouble, I thought I'd ask you about it."*

"Ok, what's the trouble?"

"I was on a workshop last year that was really good for me, and at the end of it I experienced myself as already whole. It was a real clear experience, and it really changed my life. But then it went away after a while, and part of why I came here is to get back to that place. So now I'm working on 'What am I?' and I keep trying to do that. And I can do it sometimes, but other times I can't. And now I'm not sure what to do."

"I would let go of trying to re-create any of your previous experiences. Getting involved in all that interferes in the natural process of going deeper here. Even though

that was an important experience for you on that workshop, let it be. You don't have to deny it, just let it be. Now, if you happen to experience yourself as whole at some stage here, then let it happen, but don't try to create it, or re-create it. We don't know what the next level of experience is there for you. We need to be open about that. Okay?"

"Okay, but does that mean my last experience wasn't real?"

"No, it doesn't mean that at all. It just means that previous experiences can become barriers if we hang onto them. It's best for you here to just let all your past experiences be whatever they were and contemplate fresh each time you contemplate."

"Okay, I can try that."

INTERVIEW 3:
INTENDING TO *DIRECTLY* EXPERIENCE

Mischka, aged thirty-seven: *"I'm working on 'What am I?' and I thought I'd just check in with you about my technique."*

Master: *"Okay, what are you doing now with your technique?"*

"Well, I get this sense of myself, here now. And then I try to be centered. Then I say what happened."

"Ah. Instead of trying to be centered, intend to experience yourself directly."

"But how can I make progress if I'm not centered?"

"Ask, with intention, 'What is it that's trying to center itself?' Because that's you. Keep reaching into the essence of that, intending to experience your true nature directly, not through any activity of centering. Go for directly experiencing that which can be centered or off center or not concerned about being centered. I'm not saying it's easy, but that's where to put your efforts."

"So it doesn't matter if I'm centered or not?"

"Let centering occur naturally, or not, in this process. Sometimes we get off center in this work. It happens. You might get flustered or irritable or whatever, and it's important to let your experience be whatever it is. In those moments, intend to directly experience what it is that's off center, that's flustered, or whatever. Let being centered occur or not occur. Just put all your efforts into trying to directly experience what you are, whether you are centered or not."

"I see, alright, I'll try it."

INTERVIEW 4:
AN OUTSIDE PROBLEM

Sometimes a person has concerns from the outside that are genuine problems distracting him or her from attending fully to the Enlightenment Intensive:

Anthony, aged thirty-seven: *"You know, I just realized I have to make a really crucial communication to my business partner today, or we could be in a lot of trouble come Monday. Can I just go do that? Then I can let go of all that for this weekend."*

Master: *"Is it something simple a monitor could do for you?"*

"Well . . . there might be some question about it . . . I'd rather do it myself, and make sure it's fully complete."

"Okay, I'll have a monitor take you to the phone on the next break. Go ahead and make the call, and then return to your question here."

"Okay, good, thank you."

INTERVIEW 5:
IT'S A GUY THING

Jim, aged twenty-eight: *"Something keeps coming up for me. Ah . . . Notre Dame is playing Miami today, and it's a huge game. Huge. And I can sort of feel it happening right now, in the cells of my body, actually, as I sit here, you know? Do you think we could have a monitor just check the score on that?"*

Master: *"Oh, let go of the game for now. Stay working on your question."*

"How 'bout later on around dinner if you just tell me who won. Just who won. I don't need to know the score or any details."

"What question are you working on here?"

"Who am I?"

"If you have trouble setting the game aside, then use that energy for your contemplation. Who is it that likes college football? Who wants to know who won? Who am I, that has this urge to know? Keep trying to directly experience that one. That's the place to put all your efforts right now."

"Oh God, I don't know if I can forget about that game, I've been watching Notre Dame my whole life."

"Well, I understand. I like football too but it's not going to work for us to divide our energy this weekend. You don't need to try to forget about football. Being into football is real for you, so let it be, it's okay. We just don't want to feed it because all you will end up with is more football that way, and here we're working on who you are. So just keep working on 'Who am I?' and if thoughts about the game come up, then express them fully to your partner. If you take this approach then this thing about the game will gradually recede. And after we end Sunday night you can go find out all about it."

"All right . . . but this is a real sacrifice, you know."

"I understand."

On an Enlightenment Intensive, people give up cigarettes, TV, and all sorts of other things for the three days. It is necessary, in order to reduce the distractions and create the focus. This young man wasn't completely happy with the response he got, but after a while the whole matter passed as he got more deeply into the world of his contemplation. As one can imagine, to accommodate all the urges people have would lead to a very diluted version of the Enlightenment Intensive.

INTERVIEW 6:
LEARNING TO CONTEMPLATE THE ACTUALITY OF ONESELF

Master: *"How's it going?"*

Jurgen, aged forty-three: *"Slow, and I'm not sure if I'm doing it right."*

"What's the question you're working on?"

"Who am I?"

"All right, when your partner says, 'Tell me who you are,' what do you do?"

"Well, I say to myself, 'Who am I?' and then I see what there is to say."

"Are you communicating everything that you notice to say?"

"Yeah, but everything seems so dry now, like I could talk on and on and not get anywhere."

"Do you get a sense of yourself when you contemplate, or do you just say the question to yourself?"

"I mainly say the question."

"Well, that's all right for the beginning, but I would add this now: start each contemplation by trying to notice yourself. You are the asker of the question 'Who am I?' Go for who is asking the question. It's you. Keep reaching for that one each time you contemplate now. You have a sense of what I mean?"

"Uh . . . not exactly."

"All right, well, you are looking at me now, right?"

"Yes."

"Okay, go ahead and keep looking at me, and at the same time try to notice yourself, the one who is looking."

". . . Ah, oh, I see."

"So each time you contemplate, try to notice you, first. And contemplate yourself, okay?"

"Okay, I'll try it."

"All right, good."

INTERVIEW 7:
LEARNING TO CONTEMPLATE THE ACTUALITY OF LIFE

Petra, aged thirty-one: *"I'm working on 'What is life?' and I feel like I'm just going around in circles."*

Master: *"All right, what do you do when your partner gives you your instruction?"*

"Well, I say to myself, 'What is life?' And then I wait and see what comes up. Then I say it. Usually I get some memory about my life, or some theories I learned in biology. I really can't see spending three days doing that."

"Neither can I. Here's how to go now. Each time you contemplate, first choose a piece of life, something that to you is life. It doesn't matter what it is as long as, to you, it's a part of life itself. It could be the rug or your hand or the tree outside the window. It could be any part of life. Then contemplate that. Okay?"

"Really? I don't know what to pick."

"Well, pick a piece of life here, now."

"Ah . . . well, the sunlight coming through the window over there is part of life."

"Okay, good. So, when you contemplate now, first notice that sunlight over there and try to directly experience what it is. Always use some actual part of life when you contemplate."

"Okay. But what if I notice something else as being life?"

"Go ahead and contemplate it. You may stay on one thing for a while, or go from this to that. The important thing is to be contemplating life itself. Okay?"

"Okay! I'll try it!"

"Good."

Life in all its forms is too vast for people to work on in the beginning. The tendency in the beginning is to "mentalize" it and move away from the reality rather than toward it. The path to enlightenment is in the direction of the reality, of facing it again and again.

INTERVIEW 8:
CONTEMPLATING TOO INTELLECTUALLY, WITH NO REALITY INVOLVED

Ben, aged thirty-six: *"Could I trouble you for a moment of your time?"*

Master: *"Sure, what's up?"*

"Well, I've been trying to understand the phenomenology of what we're doing here. And it seems to me that what we're really grappling with here is the whole field of ontology. And if we're talking ontology, then as far as I'm concerned we're talking Heidegger. And, frankly, I'm not hearing anyone come up with anything he didn't already come up with . . . I'm also hearing a lot of pretty off-the-wall stuff too . . . I mean, you obviously have no educational requirements for taking an Enlightenment Intensive . . . "

"Just go for who it is that's thinking, okay? Otherwise you're just going to get three days of thinking."

"So I am to think about the thinker?"

"Not exactly. Ask yourself, 'Who am I, that's thinking right now?' and try to experience it directly. Ask, 'Who is conscious of my thoughts?' and go for directly experiencing that one. It's you. Can you try to reach past your thinking processes like that, as best you can, each time you contemplate?"

" Uh . . . mmm, that sounds radical . . . well, I'll go give it a try."

INTERVIEW 9:
DOING FINE

Sometimes a participant is right on track and needs no correction at all, just some validation of the direction and some encouragement to go on:

Roberto, aged forty-two: *"I just thought I'd check in to see if I'm doing this right."*

Master: *"Okay, what are you doing now when you work on your question?"*

"Well, I'm working on 'What is another?' And I usually use my dyad partner to contemplate . . . and I just put my attention on them as they are, and I try to directly experience them. And I let myself be open to how that effects me and what it brings up in me. Then I communicate that."

"All you need to do is keep at that. You're right on track. Don't hold back."

"Okay . . . thanks."

10:
I ALREADY KNOW WHAT LIFE IS.

Master: *How's it going?*

Claudia, aged forty-five: *"Well, I'm working on 'What is life?' and the problem is I already know what life is. It's the present moment. It's simple. But we make it complex."*

"Well, there may be some truth to what you're saying, but are you directly conscious of it?"

"Well, I've known that life is the present moment for a long time."

"I suggest you go deeper. If you are noticing the present moment, try to directly experience what it is. What is a present moment? What's its true nature? Okay, there's the present moment, but what is that? Is it a thing, or what? There's a whole world there for you to discover. I suggest you go for that."

"Well, I've been okay with the fact that life is the present moment. I never looked at it any deeper. I don't know what the true nature of the present moment is; it just is."

"Well, you can leave it at that, or go deeper. Because there is deeper to go if you want."

"Well, now you've got me curious. But if I look more deeply into the present moment, won't that take me out of the present moment?"

"It might, but so what? Sometimes to find the deeper truths we have to go in and out of the present moment. You might have to process out old memories, for example. And anyway, in a direct experience there is no present moment. You've transcended the present moment. There is no 'present' and there is no 'moment.' So if you are hanging onto the present moment or to anything else, it's going to hold you up in this work. For here, I would just go for the true nature of what life is, and let yourself go through whatever you have to go through, be it past, present, future, or no time at all."

"Okay, I'll try that."

Interviews are important points of instruction, clarification, contact and support. They add to the support found in the dyad process itself, the general lectures and the presence of the monitors. Many people will look back and see that an interview at some point on the way was crucial in getting them going in the right direction, or keeping them going.

ON THROUGH THE SECOND DAY: THE AWAKENING OF THE ENERGIES OF TRUTH

The way to the way it is,
is to follow the way it is in you.
—Russell Scott

THROUGHOUT THE SECOND DAY, most people are communicating and sharing more unself-consciously, safely held within the container created by the dyad structure, the rules, and the staff's support. Things get more real. People are less cautious, more involved in working on their question, more intent on just expressing what's coming up. This is necessary. How can reality be experienced directly if things are kept unreal and superficial? This process gradually frees up hidden energies. These could be called the energies of truth. They awaken in different ways for different people.

AUTHENTICITY IN RELATING

The most common way the energies of truth begin to release on an Enlightenment Intensive is through this continuing process of each person telling more of the honest truth about him or herself. It's really that simple. Gradually there is more authentic sharing and from this, new energy begins to awaken and move within each individual. Forms of chronic tension may begin to dissolve. The subtle stress of having to be a certain way in life begins to evaporate. Saying what's so in a non-abusive environment has a way of awakening and moving energy in a person that is relieving. This energy isn't being forced to awaken and move, it just naturally tends to do so when the truth is being shared hour after hour.

IRRITABILITY OR UPSET

The energies of truth may awaken as irritability or upset. A person may have spent the greater part of the first day unconsciously being a good boy or a good girl, like in school. But, as that approach leads nowhere, the deeper truths begin to arise into consciousness. Finally, one may hear something like: "God *dammit*, I'm just sitting here being good, like I've been my whole life!" Or: "I've never told my boss how much he irritates me. He *really* irritates me! I've just been stuffing it down for five years."

REMEMBRANCES OF THE HEART

The energies may begin to awaken as soft emotions arising from the heart: "I just keep thinking about this dog I had, who died when I was twelve. I just really loved him; I'd sort of forgotten how much . . . " There may arise the humming of an old, heartfelt tune that once had great meaning and has now come up as a result of contemplating.

ROMANTIC OR EROTIC PASSION

The contact in the dyads and the truth shared can have the effects of an aphrodisiac: "My old girlfriend keeps coming up when I contemplate now. She was so beautiful. I can feel these hands of mine just wanting to reach out and touch her."

Many people report that at some point others begin to look more attractive, more real, and more sexy, not from any particular behavior but from somehow just in the way they are. Of course, this opens up the opportunity for people to begin getting involved in romantic or sexual interests. The structure, the rules, and the guidance of the staff all support participants to not suppress such energy but at the same time to not make communications that involve their partners directly. In this way the energies are neither suppressed nor allowed to run wild. Instead, they are channeled into enlightenment work.

No one should not try to make these energies happen, since that effort then becomes an interference in the natural process. In the natural process, the normally hidden or repressed energies in the body, mind, and emotions begin to surface on their own as a side-effect to one's work on the Enlightenment Technique. Therefore, one's efforts are always best put only into the Enlightenment Technique, and not into anything else.

SPONTANEOUS SHAKINGS

Energy may arise for some in the form of spontaneous jerkings or shakings in the body. It can feel like the universe is rumbling deep inside. This is a phenomenon well known to Yoga meditators and sitters of *zazen*. The person may feel like a volcano or an earthquake and may be very surprised by the spontaneous nature of the event.

PASSION FOR TRUTH

Sometimes one begins to realize, "I want the truth. I really want it. Before, I sort of wanted it, but now I want it." Now, the passion for the truth can arise with new power. It tends to put a person into a whole other energy state, a condition more mobilized, spontaneously interested, and purposeful.

HUMOR AND HYSTERICS

Remembrances of funny times may ambush the consciousness, seizing its attention in a kind of high-energy excitement that is surprising considering that no alcohol is being served: *"OH, MY GOD, I remember the time when I was a kid, a few days before Christmas, I stole one of my brother's shoes. He looked everywhere for it! Then I wrapped it up and put it under the tree for him to open on Christmas morning!"* This, followed by rocking peals of laughter. After a bit, the memory and humor pass, and the person quiets down and returns to his contemplation. And now he brings to bear on it a whole new flow of freed-up life energy.

People don't normally recognize these signs as the awakening of the energies of truth, as signs that the energy centers of their body are opening. These awakening energies may even cause confusion in anyone who arrives believing that contemplation is always peaceful and quiet and never passionate or robust.

The energies of truth are peaceful and quiet sometimes, but sometimes they are passionate and robust. Sooner or later, these awakening energies begin to educate people in one way or another that going after direct experience sometimes involves the earthy forces of our human nature; that the way to truth itself is not the path of avoiding or suppressing these energies, but the path of letting them awaken. Then, without rushing to the refrigerator or striking out at others or lunging for a sex partner, pouring that energy into the task of direct experience. This way requires some kind of  a container and a support system, such as the Enlightenment Intensive provides. Otherwise the seeker, experiencing the onset of these awakening energies, will tend to dissipate them through dramatic acting out, or will knock them back down to a safe, tolerable level through overeating or overworking or oversomething.

As the normally sleeping energies begin to awaken, barriers usually come up. On the one hand, some kind of energy is awakening that wants to put us more deeply into reality than we've ever been. On the other hand, we have fixed mental, emotional, and physical tendencies that protest this revolution in consciousness that is starting to happen. At this stage, education about the barriers to enlightenment is extremely useful, often crucial, for helping people get through them.

SECOND DAY LECTURE:
THE BARRIERS TO ENLIGHTENMENT

The path into the light seems dark.
The path forward seems to go back.
—Lao-tzu

NOW IS A GOOD TIME for you to hear about the barriers to enlightenment, otherwise they can stop you. These barriers have been well known in meditation systems for centuries, so there is nothing I'm going to say here that is new. Being educated about them in advance is important because it takes away a lot of the hidden power these barriers can seem to exert. Once you know about them you can recognize them when they come up, and you can just keep going instead of buying into them. In practical terms the barriers to enlightenment come in three main categories: mental, emotional and physical. There is also one final barrier which is not in any of those categories.

MENTAL BARRIERS: THE THOUGHT POLICE

One mental barrier in this work is what you might call the "Thought Police." Suppose something socially unacceptable starts to come up in your mind, like thoughts of power or violence or sex or greed or revenge, or something like this, and you go to say it but before you do, this other thought comes in and says, "You better not say that." So you don't say it. Sometimes the Thought Police are so repressive as to also say, "Don't even think it." Then your process is held up because you are back being a nice social person instead of saying what's actually coming up.

The way to handle the Thought Police is to first differentiate between thoughts and actions. If you have the thought, "I want to smash that window," it doesn't mean you have to go do it. In fact, don't do it. It would just create more distraction. Instead of continuing to work on enlightenment, we'll be bandaging your hand and fixing the window and wasting a lot of time. Acting out like that doesn't work. But total repression doesn't work either. So the thing to do is the third way, the healthy way: honestly feel and express these thoughts in the dyad, but don't act them out. If you have great difficulty communicating on a particular subject to your partner, come say it to me and it will remain private between us.

This is a process of letting what is there be there, whatever it is, dark or light. Sometimes people suddenly realize this: "Wow, this really is about the truth here." Yes, it is. As your boldness increases to embrace just what is, and you become more able to stay within the safe container of the dyad structure, then these thoughts and feelings can be processed out. They can be transformed out of the endless cycles of repression and acting out that never really go anywhere. And then the deeper reality of your true nature can finally be known.

PRECONCEIVED IDEAS

Of the mental barriers, preconceived ideas are the most insidious and the most pervasive. A preconceived idea is the holding on to an idea and projecting it onto reality. For example, suppose I'm working on what I am and I have the idea, "What I am is a man." Okay, well, maybe it's true. I do have a male body. But maybe in terms of my true nature it's partly true and partly not true. Or maybe it's completely not true. I don't know, so I really ought to be open here, instead of holding onto this idea. This idea becomes a barrier only if I hold onto it. If I do that, I'm going to be subtly influencing my whole process, because if something comes up which might suggest that I'm something other than a man, I may tend to discount that, and keep making my idea being the most important thing. What I end up with in this case is not enlightenment but my idea.

It's important in this work to appreciate this point. There is, for example, the idea of an apple. You could have a totally correct idea of an apple in your mind. But you can't physically bite into it. You can only bite into an actual apple. There is a big difference here. It is very unlikely that you have any actual apples in your mind or in your brain. There may be correct ideas of apples, but nothing we can make a real pie with.

So as a technique for enlightenment, getting your favorite idea of what you are, and then hanging onto it, is very, very slow, because it's not in the universe in which real progress can be made. It's in the universe of your mind. Part of being open in this approach we are using here is to let go of preconceived ideas, even your dearest-held ones. You might say, "Well, I've always thought of myself as a good person, you don't want me to let go of that do you?" Yes, I do. I don't mean flip to the opposite and become bad; I mean just let go of the idea. If it's the truth that you are good, then that will remain all by itself; you won't have to hold on to it as an idea. And if something else is the truth, then you'll be able to experience that because you're not hanging onto an idea.

We already have our ideas. What we want more of is reality itself. We want real apples, not mental ones. To do this we have to get our own ideas out of the way and to let reality be what it actually is.

The way to get through preconceived ideas is, whenever you notice yourself hanging on to one, simply communicate it and let go of it. You don't have to denounce it, or make it wrong, just let it go as an idea, so you can look more clearly at the reality. Do this with any idea, even the ones you know absolutely for sure are correct. In fact, especially let go of those. This is one form of being open. You may have ideas from God knows where, ideas like, "I'm no good, I'm great, I'm special, I'm not special, I'm not going to get enlightened, I am going to get enlightened," and so on. You may even strongly believe some of them. Just communicate them to your partner, and then try to be more open. That's what you do with a preconceived idea.

OVERLOOKING THE OBVIOUS

There are different variations of mental barriers. They mostly boil down to preconceived ideas. One of these is overlooking the obvious. We tend to overlook the obvious because we have preconceived ideas that something else should be there besides what is actually there. In this work, it really pays to notice the obvious, to notice just what's so. So try to notice the obvious, of what you're feeling, about what the truth is for you, about what you really have to say. This is a skill you can develop, and it helps a lot.

THE BARRIER OF TOLERATING

Try not to tolerate or endure things that come up. We start to tolerate or endure when we have the subconscious idea that we can't be in the truth here, now, but have to tolerate the moment and have fulfillment later. We tend to develop preferences: "I don't want what's happening to be happening, I want something else to be happening." Yet, what's happening is what's happening. So if you notice yourself enduring something, like how angry you actually feel, or how frustrated you feel, or how irritated you are that things aren't how you want them, well, stop. Go ahead and express what's really going on with you. Don't we all know that the truth can be extremely irritating sometimes? It has no regard whatsoever for our sick and neurotic preconceived ideas or our personal preferences. Are we going to take this lying down? Are we going to just sit here and meekly let the truth be what it is, without putting up a fight? No, sir. So, express yourself. Let the truth out. Just stay in the format, and don't lay trips on your partners, so that this energy goes in the right direction.

EMOTIONAL BARRIERS

Emotional barriers are any reluctance on your part to feel any feelings that might come up. You might start to feel anger, sadness, fear, love, or some other emotion. You might start to enter the world of feelings in general, in some new way, some way that you aren't used to. Your feeling equipment may be rusty from disuse at these deeper levels. Sometimes, you can tell that the feelings are there, but you may have difficulty feeling and expressing them. Just express what you can of them, as best you can. Feelings are to be felt. In the dyad, don't aim the feelings at your partner personally. Just express them as fully as you can, and keep working on your question.

Fear in all its overt and subtle forms is one of the biggest barriers in this work. The fear can be about lots of things: fear of change, of being ridiculed, of being noticed or standing out, of rejection, exposure, and so on. It's just safer to hide out.

Feelings are a barrier when we become afraid to feel them, or when we force them and try to make them be more than they naturally are. Sometimes people think growth isn't happening unless heavy emotions are going on, but in this work that's not the case. Feelings are different from enlightenment. They are two completely different things. But feelings may come up for you at some stage when you go after enlightenment.

PHYSICAL BARRIERS

Suppose every time you contemplate who you are you get an awful, nauseous sensation in your stomach. And every time you stop contemplating who you are, the nausea goes away. Well, that's a physical barrier. It's something in your particular process that's coming up as a result of you actually reaching into who you are. If it causes you to drop your contemplation in some way, then it has acted as a barrier for you. It has become something to overcome, to not buy into, to not let stop you.

So what you do is you let the nausea come up and just be there. And while it is being there you keep working on "Who am I? Who is it who has this nausea?" And you feel and express it, not trying to overdramatize it but also not trying to tough your way past it stoically. Let the thing be. If it hurts a little, say, "It hurts a little." If it's making you want to vomit, then say, "It's making me want to vomit." Then go right back to "Who am I?" We'll bring a wastebasket over to you if you want, although it's not usually needed. Usually once the thing is experienced out, it passes, and you are beyond that barrier.

Some people have almost no physical barriers come up for them. Others have big ones: headaches, creeping sensations in the skin, fever—it can be almost anything. Energy rushes, visual distortions, and so on. Physical barriers are not something that have to happen. They may happen, and they may not.

A monitor (center) will sometimes go into a dyad to give support or guidance.

THE FINAL BARRIER

There's one final barrier to enlightenment, and it's a total one. There may come a time when you've covered all the ground there is to cover, you've gotten through your mental, emotional and physical barriers, and yet you reach a point where no more forward progress can be made. It's as if you've walked all the way from the East Coast of America and you hit the Pacific Ocean. No more walking is possible. Yet you aren't having a direct experience. But the truth itself is right there, at your fingertips, you can sniff it in the air and almost taste it. It draws the attention, but at the same time you are not in union with it.

At that stage, what to do is to stop walking and sit down. There is no more getting any closer. You're there, you're just not in union. And what you do while you are sitting there is you intend to be directly conscious of that actuality. We cannot make the union happen; that is why this barrier is total, in terms of our own efforts to get past it. But what we can do is not back off. We can keep sitting there, intending to be one with it, being open to whatever it might be, communicating what's coming up. We can do this instead of going back over old material or telling jokes or getting involved in some other activity. And at some point enlightenment may occur, through what in human terms can only be called a miracle. That is the last barrier to enlightenment.

Whatever's going on for you at this stage, try to notice if you've internally backed off. We have the ability to quietly back off the technique and just park ourselves in some safe part of the mind and listen to music for a while, or think about other things, things that are easier to confront. Every time you can get yourself to come back around and face yourself, life, or another, every time you do that, you are progressing. Keep at that as hard as you can, and apply anything you've learned here about getting through the barriers.

The whole subject of the barriers to enlightenment can be discussed at great length. The master doesn't take the time to go into them all but will give general advice about the most common ones and will help people on an individual basis as necessary. For example, inspired creative urges can surge up like a fever, driving the person to secretly go off and scribble notes for future books, systems of thera-py, plans for saving the world, or whatever. There's nothing wrong with this. It's not a moral or ethical issue. It's a matter of staying on purpose. Thus a person experiencing this will be guided back to the dyad to stay at his technique, to keep going for a real result in terms of direct experience.

Powers can be a barrier. Suppose a person suddenly begins knowing people's thoughts, or seeing their auras, or their past lives, or having cognitions of the future. These powers become distractions if the person drops his or her contem-plation and becomes fascinated with them, or if the ego starts swelling with self-importance and the idea of being different and better.

For all of these things, the answer is essentially the same: don't try to make them happen or keep them from happening. Keep working on the question.

Any master experienced at giving Enlightenment Intensives will be a good source of war stories about supporting people up against the barriers to enlighten-ment. These barriers can come up from any quarter, at any time. What is it like to be going along on an Enlightenment Intensive and to come up against unknown barriers? In the next chapter is an account of someone who faced, and got through, some significant barriers in her first Enlightenment Intensive.

FACING THE FIRE,
AND BREAKING THROUGH: AN ACCOUNT

TARA

TARA IS BRITISH and spoke with me in 1984 about the barriers she faced on her first Enlightenment Intensive. Her account is a good example of someone encountering the barriers of fear and aloneness, and getting through them:

I took my first Enlightenment Intensive here in England in 1981. On the first day I had a headache and a backache, and generally felt really irritable. One of the main things I had to confront was a fear of going crazy. Every time I asked myself, "Who am I?", there was this hollow fear feeling in my stomach that it really wasn't ok to open up to who I am. But I felt that something real was happening in the midst of it all, so I kept working at my question and communicating what was coming up.

It may at first glance sound terrible that the poor girl was suffering and that the Enlightenment Intensive was somehow doing this to her. But these kinds of barriers are not created by the Enlightenment Intensive, they are simply exposed. What we really need in our growth process is not more hiding from our inner barriers but spaces in which they can be experienced, expressed and got through. What Tara was experiencing was an essential part of her unique unfoldment.

On the morning of the third day, I was out on walking contemplation. And I realized for the first time that on some basic level in life, I am alone. And I just howled. The walk ended and I went back into the dyad, and I kept howling and sobbing over this realization that I am, basically, alone. My whole body was involved, every cell. Finally it passed, and I went back to work on my question. And some time later I had a direct experience. It was associated with a very body experience. Something seemed to explode somewhere in my solar plexus region and radiate through my body. It was bliss . . . pure joy. The nearest thing to it was something like being cold and sipping a hot drink, but in this case the warmth was coming out from inside my body.

These physical sensations that Tara experienced were not the actual direct experience itself but the side effects. The side effects are not predictable, and they vary a lot from one person to the next. Beginners in enlightenment work sometimes think these surprising effects are the enlightenment itself, and that what we are trying to do is create these special effects. This is a serious error. An enlightenment experience may trigger side effects such as Tara experienced, but it also may not. Either way, the enlightenment breakthrough itself is nonphysical in nature:

I directly experienced that I, in fact, am. I'm not a figment of my imagination or anything. I, in fact, am. This experience didn't last long, but it completely affected my experience of myself and my life from then on. At the time I was filled with love and happiness, and all my physical discomforts went away. And ever since then my lower back has been looser. I think some sort of thawing took place, and I don't know what it was about and it doesn't really matter to me. What matters for me is the fact that I am. I had never realized that before.

In some therapeutic systems, Tara's emotional catharsis out on the walk might have been considered a result in itself. On the Enlightenment Intensive, it's just something else coming up to be communicated and expressed so that, in this case, the "Who am I?" question can be worked on more deeply, more truly. This is a vital distinction between normal therapeutic processes and the enlightenment project. People do not have to go through an emotional catharsis in order to have a enlightenment experience, but it is not uncommon.

After the Intensive I felt full up for the first time in my life. I kept remembering the Biblical saying "My cup runneth over," because that fit exactly how I felt. I'd never felt that before. I had always had a hollow, empty feeling that I tried to fill with relationships, cigarettes, food, anything, and for the first time I didn't feel the need to fill myself up with anything. I was full. And some part of that feeling has never gone. I can still have an empty feeling, but it doesn't have the same desperate quality to it anymore. And I have never felt suicidal since that time. I used to think about killing myself a lot back then, because I couldn't stand life. Now I would never kill myself.

Not everyone has such a time as Tara did. But there are real barriers in this work, sometimes challenging ones, and this is a fact people should know about. One advantage is that these barriers come up organically from one's own efforts at working on the question. They are not provoked by a staff person shouting at people, for example. And they come up inside the container of the Enlightenment Intensive, in which a complete support system exists for going through them.

It comes as some surprise to people who continue to take Enlightenment Intensives to find that each time they take one the barriers may be different. In fact, their whole experience of being there may be different. Tara's story is not unusual in this.

The next Intensive I did was completely different. I didn't have a direct experience, but I kept wanting everybody else to have one rather than me. And then, on the way home, I asked myself the question, "Who am I?" and a very calm, quiet knowingness of who I am was there. It didn't feel like the previous direct experience, it was just as if the knowledge had been sitting there, and I had always known it, and had glanced 'round and become conscious of it. The other experience had all the fireworks, but this one didn't. It was very quiet. And it had a quality of God in it.

Some people come to an Enlightenment Intensive thinking that enlightenments are always explosive events. This is not the case, and such a preconceived idea can interfere in the natural process. The best policy is to go for the truth itself and be open. In Tara's case, she ran into something completely unexpected:

I had been a Marxist for years and had angrily rejected God and religion, seeing them as destructive and oppressive. But in that experience, it was as if a door had opened. And the door was the possibility of God as a reality, as opposed to a theory or a belief or the trappings of religion. When I went to bed that night I was lying there, and for the first time in my life I had a conversation with God. And I said, "Maybe sometime . . . ."

The awakening of religious feelings is a highly personal thing. On an Enlightenment Intensive it certainly does not occur for everyone.

The practical, in-life benefits of a direct experience are always unpredictable. Such a breakthrough sometimes transforms an unexpected part of life:

My relationship with my father completely changed after that. Experiencing who I really am let me give up the position of rebellious daughter, and that let him give up his position of domineering father, so we both gained. We really like and love each other now. If I had never gotten anything else out of Enlightenment Intensives, having a good relationship with my father would have made it all worthwhile. And I am really in life now. Before, I'd been very self-destructive and I knew that if I didn't find something to change how I dealt with my life, I'd die young. What I've gotten out of Enlightenment Intensives is the main contributing factor now to my wanting to live, to knowing that life is okay."

The barriers to enlightenment can be formidable, no matter what system is used. Tara was fortunate to have the right kind of persistence and willingness to express herself, which enabled her to process out the barriers that came up for her. In the dyad system of the Enlightenment Intensive, communication and self-expression play a unique and important part in this processing. How does this work?

10

COMMUNICATION IN THE DYADS: HOW AND WHY IT WORKS

FOR MANY PEOPLE, it's not obvious at first how this dyad format can possibly be effective for the purpose of enlightenment. It just looks like two people sitting there talking. To understand the dyad format, we have to first look at the role of the mind in the enlightenment project. The chattering mind, with all its monologuing, concepts, desires, and judgments, is the principle obstacle to enlightenment regardless of the tradition or technique used. One way or the other, the mind must be broken out of in order to have a real possibility to directly experience the true self. What can be done to win this inner battle?

SILENCE AND MEDITATION: THE TRADITIONAL WAYS OF DEALING WITH THE MIND

Who we are is not the concepts in our mind, nor its judgments, nor any part of it at all. The ancient masters knew this from their own direct experience. But just saying this to their students wasn't enough. The students, without any direct experience of their own, couldn't help but immediately conceptualize this information and simply add it into their thinking. So the masters developed meditation techniques, often based on what they themselves did that worked, to help their students get beyond their mind and directly experience who they really are.

These ancient approaches usually call first of all for silence. Silence tends to still the mind. In this context, students practice a technique designed to break the mind's hold on them. One of these techniques teaches you to put your attention onto your breath and watch only that. Another teaches that whenever a thought arises, you say to yourself, "Not that." Some use a repetitive, mind-breaking question such as, "Does a dog have Buddha-nature?" Many teach to continually repeat a phrase or word, such as "One." A particularly brutal approach teaches you to sit facing a blank wall. The mind, after a session or two of this kind of treatment, begins to violently object. As the meditator persists in sitting after sitting, the mind rears up in full flight and goes through its thrashings and clamorings and convincing arguments about why it would be better to go do anything other than sit facing this blank wall. The fortunate contemplator who is able to do well at this blunt object approach will eventually experience the mind exhausting itself down to nothing. This opens the door to the profound emptiness and divine union possible in the realms beyond.

There are a lot of other techniques. One of their shared characteristics is a long sitting in silence. This makes these techniques especially difficult for restless Westerners when they are practiced for anything more than an hour or so a day.

Now, there is another way to deal with the content of the mind: communicate it out.

COMMUNICATION

It's a universal human experience that when you've got something on your mind and you get it across to someone else, you are in some way unburdened. Somehow in that process, if the communication was successful, whatever was on your mind leaves.

Every mother knows that once she has received and understood the concerns of her child about what happened that day, then her child can let go of them and sleep in peace. Yet, the peaceful sleep of a child is a thing unknown to many adults,

and a major reason is the stack of unresolved communications that are still held in the mind at the end of the day. Dreams become agitated or inaccessible. One wakes not rested but as if from a struggle, or as if from under anesthesia. Why? In simple terms, it is because of the inner turmoil in the conscious and subconscious parts of our mind that arises from all our unexpressed thoughts and feelings.

THE CONDITION OF THE LIE

The social structure in which we live and our own particular fears and restraints all conspire, if we let them, to make liars out of us. I often work with people who have problems in their family, work, or relationship, and the single greatest cause of all of these problems is that the truth isn't being told or lived, it's being withheld. When the truth is uncovered and expressed in appropriate ways, only then does life begin shifting into alignment with it. Only then do people start feeling better. Most of us know what it's like to have a really good communication with someone, and then go away clearer, calmer, more in touch with our own self and with others. This is an experience that reminds us of the cleansing power of honest relating.

COMMUNICATION AND MEDITATION: A NEW WAY

In the dyad format, there is the continual opportunity for participants to express to their partner the truth of what they are thinking and feeling as a result of their contemplation. Whereas silence tends to still the mind, this particular kind of communication tends to empty and unburden the mind. When combined with repeated considering of a question like "Who am I?" participants thus begin to come more into their natural self, beyond the world of ideas, confusions and inner chatter. This in turn sets up an internal condition in which direct experience is more likely to occur. This is the great advantage of the dyad format and the essence of how it can help us win the battle with the mind. Like most activities of this nature, it must be experienced to be fully appreciated.

Why hasn't this been discovered before? What has kept the inherent power of honest communication from being widely exploited for enlightenment purposes?

The answer is simple: communication is a minefield of potential problems that can stir up the mind and get it going. There are two especially common problems.

INTERRUPTION AND JUDGMENTS

Researchers have isolated two major culprits in the breakdown of our relating: interruption and judgments.

We enter into our relating with each other armed with an arsenal of devices for showing our displeasure: snide comments, name-calling, cold silence, sarcasm, threats, smirks and other subtle gestures, to name only a few. When we use these devices, they tend not to calm or empty the mind, but to stir it up. They work to enmesh us in relationship issues instead of free us from them. Because they jam up the easy flow of understanding, their legacy is a torment of mental upset. Problems in the relating of couples spring immediately to mind here. Couples who specialize in interruption and judgment create a kind of relationship hell in which sustainable intimacy is destroyed and neither one can know any true peace. Couples who gain some mastery over these tendencies can maintain their flow of honest sharing and understanding and thus their sense of mutual caring. They create less "mind" in their relationship and can therefore have more real contact.

It's no wonder that silence and solitude have been traditionally sought as a precondition for serious self-enquiry. Under most conditions communication does tend to stir up the mind. Dyads also are not immune to the potential problems of communication, such as judgment and interruption. If you just have two people sitting down face-to-face in a dyad with no ground rules to follow, the communication will probably break down eventually. You'll get people making remarks like, "Boy, you took an awfully long time to say something during your last turn." Going in these kinds of directions, you'll end up either with ordinary conversation at best, or a fight at worst.

LISTENING WITHOUT INTERRUPTION OR JUDGMENT

But when a few simple ground rules are followed in a dyad, the dishonorable Interruption and his unsavory brother, Judgment, are kept out of the picture.

The simple rule for this is: listen silently, and speak without judging what the other has said. Under these particular conditions, the mind is not stirred up by communication, but rather is emptied, released and unburdened.

Interruption is further avoided in dyads because both partners know beforehand that they will get equal five-minute turns to speak. This is not always clear in our normal relating, so we sometimes develop anxieties about getting time for what we have to say. In a dyad, equal turns to speak are preordained, so people can relax about that point.

When these ground rules are followed in a dyad, participants gradually experience that it's safe to contemplate their question and communicate their truth, whatever it is.

COMMUNICATION AND THE SELF

In any project designed to uncover the truth of something, the opportunity to say the truth is essential. How can the truth be uncovered if the truth is not allowed to be spoken? Yet chronic, unspoken truth is the very condition in which a lot of folks arrive at the Enlightenment Intensive. Many have grown up in a situation of too much interruption and judgment. They learned to habitually withhold the fuller truths of who they are in order to avoid the pain and turmoil that went with it. This strategy may have made sense at the time, but over the long term it created a serious problem: the person gradually knew less and less about who he or she really is.

It is an observable principle of life that our intelligence on any given subject tends to rise in direct proportion to our ability to communicate freely on that subject. Thus, someone growing up in a household with a lot of open conversation about sports, but not much about politics, will tend, over time, to have a much higher intelligence quotient on the subject of sports than on politics.

Similarly, if someone grew up in an environment in which it was not all right to express freely about who he or she really is, then that person's intelligence quotient regarding who he or she is will tend to atrophy. There will be mystery, confusion and unknowingness about the self. The person's life energy will tend to go instead into the development of a sophisticated personality, or it may become entrenched in a chronic state of protest, such as sullenness. This is a truly amazing situation. You would think we would be experts on who we are, if on nothing else. What could be closer to us than who we are? But it turns out that we can actually be made ignorant on the subject of who we really are through an overemphasis on social training, the accumulation of traumatic incidents, and the lack of opportunity for real relating.

The dyad structure deliberately reverses this trend, placing the emphasis on you and your truth. When the noninterruption and nonjudgment rules are followed, the dyad cleverly avoids the problems of normal human relating, yet makes full use of our ability to sense and express our living truths. Hour after hour of this, when combined with the contemplation of the question, leads people into purer expressions of who they are, and, eventually, into direct experience.

This process can actually be observed happening. A woman named Colleen put it this way:

I was a Senior Monitor once, watching people work. And I noticed that each time someone told the truth, the space changed. It got more spacious. There was more room for the truth to enter. Each little act of telling the truth made it more possible for truth, or reality, just to be present, with or without an enlightenment experience.

It's not linear. Joe might tell a small truth that enables Mary to have a deeper experience of her own reality. Mary expressing herself in a new way might touch the core of Peter's case so much, he has an enlightenment experience. Even though Joe might not have an enlightenment experience, his truth is as important to the whole process as Peter's enlightenment. Without Joe's small truth, Peter's enlightenment experience might not have happened. The small, spoken truths are the building blocks of an Enlightenment Intensive.

Combining repeated contemplation with honest self-expression, in a synergistic group environment, has enormous healing potential that opens the way to deeper direct experiences of reality. In the next chapter are three examples of participants using this way to get through significant barriers to enlightenment.

11

WHEN ALL ELSE FAILS, EXPERIENCE AND EXPRESS THE TRUTH:

THREE BRIEF ACCOUNTS

THE SIMPLE POWER of honest self-expression is sometimes subtle, sometimes healing, sometimes extraordinary. On the hero's journey to enlightenment, this approach is sometimes a friend, sometimes a tool, and sometimes a necessary weapon in facing the physical, mental and emotional barriers that are encountered:

A PHYSICAL BARRIER
RITA (SWISS, FORTY-SIX YEARS OLD)

I had had strong headaches on a regular basis since I was nine years old. Pounding migraines. I took my first Enlightenment Intensive when I was forty-one, and I got one on the first day. I just couldn't see how it would end. I talked to the master about it, and he said to try to set it aside and if I couldn't do that, to fully express it to my partner. Well, I couldn't set it aside so I communicated about it. But by the second day, it still hadn't gone away. So I began to communicate about it even more fully than before. I really went into it, into the core of it, and began to describe it, each part of it. It was all black, and concentrated around a certain point. Then on the second evening, just before breathing exercises, while I was doing this, I felt the headache become a white point instead of a general blackness. Some kind of energy spread out from that point and a transformation took place. The pain went completely away, and I went into a flowing, easy space after that. It was like going into paradise after being in hell.

I didn't have an enlightenment experience on that first Intensive, but I never had another migraine. I also used to take pills every day for high blood pressure, but I didn't need to do that anymore. My blood pressure became normal. I did get headaches again when I took my next Enlightenment Intensives but they were not as strong, and they seemed connected mostly to coffee withdrawal. When I gave up coffee in regular life, the headaches on Intensives stopped completely. And on the fourth Enlightenment Intensive, I had my first direct experience, on "What am I?"

A MENTAL BARRIER
BILL (AMERICAN, TWENTY-EIGHT YEARS OLD)

I was on a two week Enlightenment Intensive working on "What am I?" and I really had the idea that I wouldn't get enlightened. I just couldn't do the technique as well as I thought I should. I had had enlightenment experiences on three day Intensives, but I had really worked hard on those. Here I was in another state. I was not on fire at all. I kept drifting off my question, wandering in my mind, and going into states where I didn't really care about enlightenment. And therefore, it seemed to me, I wouldn't break through. Yet I was in the middle of this two-week Enlightenment Intensive. I kept getting depressed at the whole situation, that I just didn't even have a shot. But I kept communicating all this to my partners, even though it was humiliating. And I actually did return to my question each time I contemplated.

On the thirteenth day, mushing along like this, I suddenly directly experienced what I am. I directly experienced my true nature as eternal, as no-thing whatsoever, and it was one of the biggest surprises of my life. Even apart from the experience itself, which was profound and completely pulled me out of the state I was in, it deeply affected me that I could break through even as I wrestled with all these ideas and states of no energy, no enthusiasm, and inability. The breakthrough happened even in spite of my own self-judgments. And when it happened, all that suffering I'd been going through went to noth-

ing. I still get a little emotional just remembering this. It meant that some other force was at work, a force completely independent of my mind and my own calculations. I saw that keeping at it no matter what is happening is extremely valuable under those circumstances.

AN EMOTIONAL BARRIER
ANN (CANADIAN,
FIFTY-THREE YEARS OLD)

Last year, on an Enlightenment Intensive, I was coming back from lunch on the third day and thinking, "Is there any way I'm holding back, even the tiniest, little bit?" What I found was just a "tiny little bit"; not anything I could put a name to; I could just sense that something was there. So, in the next dyad I started to communicate this to my partner, and it quickly developed into an unbearable feeling around my mother. The emotion I felt was intense; I was back in the first month of my life, and I felt that my mother hated me. It felt like my heart was breaking; my body was wracked with deep sobbing, it was so intolerable that my mother hated me, that she didn't accept me. The crisis didn't last long, it washed through me in one intense burst of emotion. I just let myself feel it, and expressed it completely to my partner. It was a full trauma release.

In the next dyad after lecture, I experienced my soul returning to my body. It entered through my toes and slowly filled me up. It was not a direct experience; however, it was one of the most significant turning points in my healing. I experienced a lot of trauma in my childhood and consequently lived with a split in myself as an adult. It was as if a part of myself lived outside of my body, and with this experience I got the missing part back, all of it.

Walking Contemplation: Who is walking? Who is looking?

After the dyad was over, I remember saying, "My who came home!" Every now and then I'll do a little check, and sure enough it is still here. I'm finally home with myself.

Not everyone goes through heavy barriers on an Enlightenment Intensive, but it is not uncommon. By the second day, the master is usually spending more time in interviews and helping people make their way down the path. Sometimes this involves helping them face barriers, sometimes clarifying points of technique, sometimes just receiving experiences that people want to share.

12

SECOND DAY INTERVIEWS WITH THE MASTER

DEALING WITH BARRIERS, FINER POINTS OF THE ENLIGHTENMENT TECHNIQUE, EXTRANEOUS ISSUES, EXPERIENCES SHARED

INTERVIEW 1:
NO MAN'S LAND—
THE BARRIER OF NOTHING COMING UP

Gunther, aged sixty-three: *"For about two hours, nothing has been coming up. I've checked very carefully and what happens is that I contemplate who I am and not a single thing comes into my consciousness. I'm just staring into space, looking. And I feel lost now."*

Master: *"Well, you may feel lost, but it's also real progress. In this place of looking at nothing, the problem is that you are the looker. If you keep looking, you'll never notice the looker. So at this point, give up trying to look, either outside yourself or inside your head. Instead, try to directly experience the looker. 'Who am I, that's looking?' Try to experience, directly, that one."*

"How do I do that?"

"I admit it's tricky. Just keep working at it in whatever way you can, reaching to the source of your looking with the intention to directly experience it. Again and again, go in that direction. You must find your own way with this. But it can be found as you keep going that way."

"Okay, I'll try it, thanks."

INTERVIEW 2:
FACING LIFE AS IT IS

Anne, aged twenty-seven, distraught, returning from walking contemplation down a country road: *"Something really disturbing happened to me out on the walk. By the side of the road up there is a dead fawn, sprawled out . . . dead . . . it must've been hit by a car. And bugs are crawling on it and it looks horrible, and I'm just extremely disturbed by this . . . I really don't want to deal with it. I was having a peaceful contemplation of what life is, and then I came upon this."*

Master: *"Life can sure get you that way sometimes."*

"Well, can't you do something about it?"

"Well, I could go remove the fawn from the side of the road, but I can't remove that part of life. Dead fawns by the side of the road being eaten by bugs are part of life, aren't they?"

"Oh, God, I don't want to deal with it . . . "

"Ah, you want to deal with just the good parts, eh?"

"I'd prefer to."

"Well, bugs and death are part of life, aren't they? How else does it make you feel?"

"I hate it. I was feeling that life is filled with love and beauty, and I thought my contemplation was going really well, when this thing happened. I feel completely thrown off track. It reminds me of watching my father get old and die . . . I just hate it."

"Go ahead into the dyad and communicate all that you're feeling to your partner, and then go right back to your question. What is life? It's that in which fawns lie dead by the road and get eaten by bugs sometimes. What is that? Try to let life in, and contemplate what it actually is, in this unpleasant aspect."

"Oh, God, all right, I'll try it, but do I have to like what life is? 'Cause there are parts I hate."

"No, that's not required, that's just something to communicate to your partners. Go ahead and express whatever comes up for you, however it makes you feel."

"Okay."

Eventually, participants working on what life is realize that life is what it is, not necessarily what we want it to be. Their contemplation then becomes more real, and deeper, but it takes a more conscious choice to go for the truth rather than one's preference.

INTERVIEW 3:
A PART OF THE TECHNIQUE UNDERSTOOD

Becky, aged sixty-one: *"I've been having real communication with my partner for what feels like the first time with anyone. I just wanted to tell you this. I remember you talking about how you should try to get yourself across to your partner, and I never really heard that. I thought I was supposed to just say what came up, like a reporter. And my partner would listen, like he was watching TV or something. And I get it now, that I'm to actually express myself to my partner. Right?"*

Master: *"That's it. You got it."*

"So this process works on real understanding?"

"Yes. When communication is fulfilled it tends to free us from what's coming up so we can go on. And it makes working on the question easier than doing it all alone."

"Great, great. [laughter] Well, I'm just going to go back and do it some more.

"Okay."

INTERVIEW 4:
A DIRECT EXPERIENCE

Janet, aged twenty-three: *"Well, something happened just earlier . . . and the monitor said I should speak to you about it."*

Master: *"What happened?"*

"I was just going along in the dyad, working on 'Who am I?', and I was listening to my partner, since it was his turn . . . and in the middle of it, this thing happened. It wasn't

really an experience; it wasn't really like anything I've ever experienced. And it really took me by surprise. I wasn't thinking about my question or anything, I was just listening to my partner. But this realization came with it, these words, that I am the truth. I'd been working hard yesterday and today, trying to experience the truth of who I am. And what I experienced is that I am the truth. I'm it! It's not like there's me, and then there's the truth of me. It's not some other thing separate from me. I'm the truth.

"Tell me more about you."

"I'm the truth. I'm it! The truth isn't some concept. I . . . me . . . I'm the truth. If someone wants the truth [laughing] they're going to have to deal with me!"

"[Laughing] I see. Okay. Tell me what else you're conscious of."

"I'm the truth itself. There's nothing else to say, really. I am the truth. I feel like I understand what Jesus was saying now in a new way, when he said 'I am the truth.' I just see it in a new way now . . . "

"Go on."

"I just keep wanting to say, 'I am the truth.' There's not me and then the truth somewhere else over there. I feel like I want to tell people, especially people who are looking for the truth. I want to tell them that they are the truth too. It's not something outside of us. It's us."

"What's being the truth like?"

"It's nothing special. It's just me. But it is special . . . it's the reality of me. I am the truth . . . [crying now] . . . and I feel like I'll always know that the truth is with me now. I won't have to worry about being separate from it, or lost . . . I mean, if I just be open to it. Right now, it's the most clear thing about me, to me, that I am the truth."

"Okay, good work. Even though you were working on 'Who am I?' you've experienced a level of what you are. Go ahead and keep being open to this actuality that you experienced, and keep communicating from it to your partners as you have been with me. Just let it roll, okay?"

"Okay."

"And then in a couple of hours come talk to me if you want about changing your question."

"OK, thanks."

It does sometimes happen that a participant will be working on one question and directly experience some other aspect of reality. This is an example of an enlightenment experience that is not explosive in terms of emotions, however it is no less real. This participant was really surprised at what she experienced, and communicated it beautifully for over an hour. Of course, her communications could be misconstrued to be egotistical, or self-deluded. In this case, they weren't. She had directly experienced an aspect of her true nature.

INTERVIEW 5:
A CASE BARRIER—THOUGHTS AND FEELINGS OF HOPELESSNESS

Michel, aged thirty-one: *"I just feel like this is hopeless. I can't get myself across to my partner and I don't think I'm contemplating very well. I just think I'm a hopeless case."*

Master: *"What question are you working on?"*

"Who am I?"

"Do you often feel hopeless in life."

"Well, usually whenever I'm doing something and it's not going well. I just think it's hopeless and I'm hopeless, and I go do something else, something I can actually do, like eat."

"Have you been communicating all these thoughts and feelings to your partner?"

"Well, somewhat. Mostly I feel hopeless and complain."

"Well, this is the stuff that's coming up when you contemplate. Intensives can be like concentrated life in the sense that whatever basic case patterns you experience in normal life may come up here in concentrated form at some stage and really try to throw you off track. So what you do is, you get this across to your partner as well as you can. These thoughts and feelings of hopelessness, they're not something to avoid, they're something to communicate to your partner. Then contemplate again. Who is this that feels hopeless sometimes and not hopeless other times? It's you. Go for that one. Don't let this thing fool you into stopping your contemplation."

"Do you think I'm hopeless?"

"No."

"These feelings really stop me in life."

"Just communicate them, and go on with your contemplation of who am I? Whenever you don't know what to do, do that. This is a barrier, a test, don't let it stop you."

". . . Okay . . . thanks."

"Good."

INTERVIEW 6:
THE BARRIER OF SOMETHING DIFFICULT TO COMMUNICATE

Jim, aged forty-one: *"There's something coming up that I don't want to go into. What should I do?"*

Master: *"What is it?"*

"Well, I'd rather not say."

"What's the main thing holding you back from saying it?"

"Well, I just think people here would think I'm weird. It might rattle their cages, too. It's also something I'm not proud of."

"Is it something that might endanger anybody here on the Intensive?"

"No, no. It's this period from my past where I did a lot of shit I shouldn't have, and I don't really want people to think I'm still into it, 'cause I'm not."

"Why don't you tell me the parts about it that you're willing to tell me, and then I'll be able to see better where to go with this."

"Well, in my twenties I did a lot of petty thieving, selling drugs, ripping people off, that kind of thing, and I did some time for it in prison. But I'm not into that stuff anymore. I got my life together after that. But when I work on what life is here, stuff from my time in prison keeps coming up, and I'm reluctant as hell to go into it out loud. Also, I don't think there's anyone here who can relate to what I'm talking about, you know? Prison is something you got to experience to know about."

"What are some of the things about it you find difficult to talk about?"

"Well, for one, there were guys in prison I liked. In a certain way, people in prison have seen parts of life other people haven't. Some of those guys know about truth in ways people here will never know."

"Well, I suggest you try to communicate this stuff to your partners here. It's okay. Go ahead and say it like you are saying it to me. Just let 'em have it. It's what's real for you, and this is what this is about. Maybe some people here will think things, but I would stand by your truth and relate it. When you talk to me about this, I can hear what you're say-ing. I can hear you. And that's the one we want here . . . Now, you don't have to. If you're totally not ready to communicate something, well don't then. But you can start by saying there's something I'm not ready to communicate, and then gradually go ahead. And if you try this, and you're really not able to progress, then come talk to me again about it, all right?"

"Okay, I'll try, but if people get freaked out about this, I'm going to let you handle them."

"It's a deal."

INTERVIEW 7:
CUPID STRIKES

Gloria, aged thirty-five: "Uh, something's happened that I didn't expect at all, and I don't know how to handle it . . . it's never happened to me before on an Intensive and I've taken four. Basically, there's this guy here who I can't stop thinking about. Yesterday we were working together in a dyad and about halfway through it I realized that with every word that was leaving his lips I was falling more and more in love with him . . . I couldn't help it . . . and it's just getting worse. I can't stop thinking about him."

Master: "Okay, well, that happens sometimes. What are you doing now when you contemplate your question?"

"I think about what to name the children we're going to have."

[Laughter] "Ok, this is serious."

"I'm just completely torn . . . I mean, basically I've had this shocking realization that I don't really want the truth, I don't really want enlightenment, I want him. And how I feel is that if this man shows any interest in me whatsoever, if he so much as smiles at me, I'm just going to follow him around for the rest of the Intensive and I don't care about the rules."

Master [laughing]: *"Okay. What question are you working on?"*

"What am I?"

"Well, falling in love happens sometimes. Under the circumstances, I wouldn't try to make this an either/or thing, like, 'either I contemplate my question or I be in love with this guy.' It will divide your energies too much and put them in conflict. Go ahead and be in love with this guy, since you are anyway, okay? And communicate this to your partners, at least the fact that you are in love. And do it in some way that he's not overhearing you and getting pulled off his question by it, okay? And see if you can contemplate what it is that's being in love. Something is, and it's you. Keep going for, 'What am I, that's in love?' What is that? This guy has awakened something in you, and you have a chance here to use this energy to make unusually deep progress with your question. Can you try this?"

"Okay, I'll try it, but I plan to get in contact with this guy after the Intensive."

"That's all up to you."

"Okay."

Gloria was eventually able to work on her question. She needed mainly to communicate more fully her real feelings about this man. In this particular case, she did contact the man after the Intensive and they dated for a while. They did not, alas, go on to live happily ever after. Feelings of love like this are sometimes seen in retrospect as illusory. Sometimes they are seen as having a sound basis for a relationship. Either way, during the Enlightenment Intensive itself, feelings like these are best communicated to someone other than the object of the attraction, such as a dyad partner or a staff person; then, going on with the question.

INTERVIEW 8:
A PURE "WHO AM I?" ENLIGHTENMENT EXPERIENCE

Helmut, aged thirty-seven: *"So what happened is that I was eating my meal at dinner, sitting alone in the backyard. And I looked at the cup in my hand. And I saw the cup, and I suddenly realized that it was me holding the cup [laughter]. It just sounds so simple, but I'd never noticed this before, like I did then. I'm the one holding my cup! It's me!"*

"Tell me more about you."

"Well, I'm the one who holds my cup! God, this sounds crazy. I can't believe I've never noticed this before. I've been holding cups most of my life, and here I am, thirty-seven years old, noticing for the first time that I'm the one holding my cup!"

[Laughter] "Go on."

"I'm me. I'm myself. I'm the one holding my cup, when I hold my cup. I'm the cup holder. I'm the one talking to you right now. Who I am is me [laughter]. It's ridiculously simple."

"Tell me more about what you're like."

"Well, I'm me! It's not complicated. I do all the things I do. I don't do the things I don't do . . . [laughter] . . . I wear the clothes I wear. I'm screwed up in the ways I'm screwed up. In the moment here I really like myself. I'm basically very likable, without adding anything."

"Okay, thank you. You've got yourself here. Now keep getting yourself across to your partners now, okay? Just present yourself as purely and as directly as you can. No hold-back, okay?"

"Okay, no hold-back. All right. Thank you."

Again, it is not the words which determine the experience here, it is the quality of the experience, difficult to capture on paper.

Continuing on through the second day and into the third, most participants begin to go more deeply into their process. Their question becomes their constant companion even as their contact with each other deepens. The third day is usually when all the work of the previous two days begins to bear the most fruit. The master will keep a steady hand on the tiller and, in the afternoon lecture, encourage people to stay with it.

THIRD DAY LECTURE: SOMETIMES, INTO DIVINE REALMS

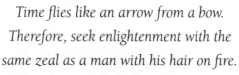

Time flies like an arrow from a bow.
Therefore, seek enlightenment with the
same zeal as a man with his hair on fire.
—Dogen Zenji

THE THIRD DAY of an Enlightenment Intensive is difficult to put into words without it sounding half-crazy. Some people are still chewing through barriers of one sort or another. Others have entered divine realms:

My heart is open, like never before. Somehow the suffering of my life is gone for now, completely. It's just nowhere to be found, even if I look for it. I feel this love for humanity.

Or:

What's coming up for me now is that I'm noticing the back of my face. I'm noticing it from the inside, sort of studying it. I'm also looking out through it. What I am is something completely separate from my face, but also somehow very involved with it.

Or:

You know, I normally feel hungry in life, and what I'm noticing now is that I don't feel hungry, I feel clean.

Or:

On the walk I was looking at this tree, and I was just completely enraptured by it, by its "isness," its beauty, the miracle of it. Somehow I was seeing it for the first time, with clear vision. It looked exquisitely sacred, like a whole religion could be based on it.

In the afternoon, lecturetime comes:

I'll say a few things about enlightenment. In an enlightenment experience, there is the event of union itself, which takes place outside of normal life experience, and there are the side effects that go with it almost simultaneously. These can be most anything: laughing, crying, surprise, shock, whatever. There can be almost no side effects at all. In terms of degree of direct experience, you might have the briefest of touches into truth itself, like going down to the lake, walking out to the end of the dock, and swishing your toe over the surface of the water. Or you might just fall in and get completely soaked. Or, you might get in a boat and spend your time rowing quietly over the surface of the lake, experiencing it's nearness and its realness, marveling at its qualities, yet remaining just outside of it. That's okay too, except we have set everything up in this Intensive in order for you to break through that last barrier into union itself. So I'll be continuing to hold a steady course in that direction.

If such a breakthrough occurs for you, if you touch into or fall into another kind of consciousness, and some aspect of reality is revealed to you, the thing to do is to present yourself. What I mean by this is to communicate *yourself* to your partners, and what you're conscious of, whatever it is. Let it be whatever it is. Sometimes people find themselves called upon by the nature of the experience to say things they would normally never say, and it can be awkward. But the more you can present yourself in unedited fashion, then the more this truth you have experienced enters your life. It becomes less of a memory and more of a stable or easily accessible part of your makeup.

In this last part of today, stay with your question. Your mind might well want to start making plans about the pizza you're going to eat, or whatever you're going to do after this is over. Try not to give that too much energy. Stay with your question and keep sharing yourself honestly with your partner about what comes up. And go as directly as you can to the actuality of whatever you are working on. Try to contact yourself, life, or another and just go for it with no mind. Want only it, for only itself. Let that passion for the truth itself release in you. It's okay to do that here. It's okay to break through into new consciousness. You have the opportunity of the ages at your fingertips.

14

THIRD DAY INTERVIEWS WITH THE MASTER: THE TOUGHER BARRIERS, AND EXPERIENCES SHARED

When where you come from
becomes where you are going
there is nothing left to ask.
—Robert Dow

THIRD DAY INTERVIEWS often involve dealing with the subtler barriers that can be holding a person up, giving encouragement, and receiving the experiences people are sharing.

INTERVIEW 1:
CONTEMPLATING TOO FANATICALLY

Peter, aged twenty-six: *"I'm just here to make sure I'm doing this right, 'cause I'm not breaking through and it's pissing me off."*

Master: *"Are you communicating all that to your partner?"*

"Yes."

"Okay, good. What are you doing now when your partner says 'Tell me what you are'?"

"Well . . . I keep trying to reach back into the source of me, to where my thoughts are coming from, to where everything about me is coming from . . . and I say to myself, 'I intend to have a direct experience, I intend to have a direct experience.' And I just hold it like that until eventually I realize I'm not having a direct experience . . . then I start to get irritated . . . and then everything goes to pieces. I really want this."

"When you contemplate now, be more open."

"Oh, God, so you think I'm forcing things too much?"

"Yes. But don't worry about it. Just be a little more open as you go on doing what you've been doing, okay?"

"Ah . . . okay, I'll try it."

INTERVIEW 2:
AN EXPERIENCE OF BEING HERE, NOW

Jason, aged sixty-two (smiling): *"Hi, I just wanted to report that I feel here, now. Normally, wherever I am in life, I don't usually feel totally here, now. Well, now, here, I do."*

Master: *"Good. Glad to have you here."*

"Thank you."

It's not a direct experience but it is a significant experience for him. There is no advice to give about these experiences, they are simply being shared as part of the unfoldment.

INTERVIEW 3:
AN ENLIGHTENMENT EXPERIENCE ON "WHAT AM I?"

Paul, aged forty-one: *"I broke through."*

Master: *"Tell me what you are."*

"I'm everything."

"Go on."

"What I am is everything. Everything that is comes out of my nature. All of it."

"Everything in this room?"

"Everything."

"Everything in the world?"

"Everything."

"Everything in the universe?"

"Everything. Everything comes from me, and everything is happening in the space of me."

""Tell me more about you."

"My nature is the source of everything. Everything is happening like . . . within me. I'm experiencing myself as vast beyond vast . . . I'm here in this body, and yet I am the space in which everything is occurring. I'm experiencing like a dual reality . . . I know I'm Paul, sitting here in front of you, and at the same time I'm conscious of this other reality. Everything that is, is happening in me. It looks like I'm this little part of life, but it's actually the opposite: all of life is in me."

"Okay. Thank you. Go ahead and keep presenting this to your partners. Keep getting across what you're conscious of, okay? Then talk to me later about changing your question."

"Okay."

As usual, in plain words, on paper, this kind of experience may appear either crazy or silly. Such experiences are far removed from everyday awareness, and make no sense in conventional terms. Yet, this is one level of direct experience that can take place for people. Certainly, no one should try to somehow generate this experience or this "answer." Other aspects of one's nature may also be experienced and in any case it is always futile to try to "create" an enlightenment experience. When actually sitting down to work on the question, one is always best off letting go of all previous experiences of others or oneself.

INTERVIEW 4:
A DIRECT EXPERIENCE ON WHAT LIFE IS

Chantal, aged forty: *"Life is."*

Master: *"Tell me more."*

"Life just is. It really is. It isn't 'isn't-ing,' it's 'is-ing.'"

"Go on."

"Life is. I can't say it any other way . . . I sit here and look around and what I see is that . . . life is. It is! Us talking together here, that is. It's something that is. It's not something imaginary, it's something that really is . . . I mean . . . I somehow never got that life really is, and now I do."

"Okay, thank you. You've opened the door to what life is. Go ahead and keep getting this across to your partners as long as you are in it, then come talk to me about either continuing on life or changing your question."

"Okay, I will."

Chantal broke through into direct experience and for the time being is not viewing reality through the filter of her mind. She is in direct contact with it, probably for the first time. The master will accept an experience like this only when he or she can detect that it is coming from the actual state of direct experience. Someone might have an insight into reality and use similar words and phrases, but it would not be enlightenment and it would not have the inherent qualities that transform consciousness at the core.

INTERVIEW 5:
THE BARRIER OF FLIGHT

Klaus, aged thirty-five (distraught and trembling): *"I've, ah . . . I've just got to go, I've gotta get out of here. I can't take this anymore, and what's happening to me."*

Master: *"What's happening to you?"*

"I just feel like I'm coming apart at the seams. I just can't be here. I've got to go. I'm sorry."

"Tell me more."

(Crying) "I just feel so alone, there's so much coming up for me . . . I can't deal with it [crying] . . . I just feel so alone in life [crying] . . . I just want to shrink up into a ball and die . . . I can't stand it . . . [crying] . . . goddammit (turning to anger), GODDAMMIT, I HATE THIS! (clenching his fists and shaking)."

Klaus continued in this way for a minute or two, the emotions pouring out of him. In these moments, the contact and emotional understanding between the participant and the master are more important than anything that is said. Finally he reached a plateau. He took a deep breath and said,

"God, I had no idea this would be this hard."

"Sometimes it can . . . I felt everything you were expressing, thank you . . .come with me back to the dyad now. I want you to continue expressing these things to your partner as you work on your question. That's the way through."

Klaus needed to express more deeply what was actually coming up for him, but he was blocked in doing that. This blocked condition tends after a while to lead to a flight response. Once through the toughest part of the barrier, he continued to express this deeper level of feelings to his partner, returning to his contemplation as the emotional charge reduced. As the charge reduced, so did any urge to leave. And he was freer now to contemplate his question more purely.

INTERVIEW 6:
PIERCING THE MYSTERY OF LIFE

Giselle, aged twenty-eight: *"I'm working on 'What is life?' And I'm having this problem, which is that it keeps dissolving. I pick an aspect of life like you said, and I go to contemplate it, and it just goes . . . empty somehow. It's hard to describe. Like I look at the rug, and I go to directly experience it, and suddenly it's sort of not real anymore, somehow not there. Visually, it's like it's not there, even though I can see it there. So I look for something that has some solidity to it, like the wall, and I try to contemplate that, and then that starts to become, like, empty too. And it's throwing me into a kind of confusion about how to contemplate this thing. I know I'm supposed to pick some part of life that's real and immediate to me . . . "*

Master: *"This point you're at now stops a lot of people, because we tend to keep wanting life to be something that our senses can grip and hold, but it starts to slip through our fingers and we get confused. Two things to do: try not to strain your senses so much by somehow trying to see into life. And try to be more open to what it is. Let the thing disappear if that's what it's going to do or somehow be here and not be here all at the same time. Let it do whatever. Meanwhile, you keep being open to what it actually is. Let it reveal its truth to you. Okay?"*

"Okay, I'll try that."

INTERVIEW 7:
THE ONSET OF PHENOMENA,
MIXED WITH PSYCHIC ABILITIES

Luke, aged thirty: *"I, ah . . . I just feel really smashed right now. I feel like my brain is short-circuiting. I was seeing my partner's face take on different shapes and shit . . . I mean, she was just sitting there listening to me, but I was seeing her face like go to wax, and then dissolve, and then become like old, and then young . . . I started to see into her future, or maybe it was her past, I don't know. I was getting all this material about her, why she's here in this life, what she's working on, trying to complete. I was just seeing it. I wasn't trying to see it, I just couldn't help but notice, you know? And it's tricky because I don't think I should start communicating about her, to her."*

Master: *"That's correct, don't go into telling her about her. Well, this kind of thing can happen, the strange phenomena, or the psychic perceptions. Basically, let them be. They may tempt you and impress you, but don't be fooled into following them. Stay with your question. Okay?"*

"Okay, but it's really affecting me that I can see into people now. I never really believed in this stuff before."

"Go ahead and communicate in general terms what's occurring for you, without getting personal about it with your partner. But return to your question rather than chase after the powers. After the Intensive you can look more into this kind of thing if you want. But here, you'll do best in terms of what we are here for by letting it be and not doing anything special with it."

"Alright. Thanks."

INTERVIEW 8:
A DENIED DIRECT EXPERIENCE

It may seem odd, but it is possible for a person to have a direct experience and deny it so quickly that it is not even recognized as such. This does not usually happen with deeper experiences. But it can happen in the beginning stages. For one thing, the experience may in no way fit the person's preconceived ideas of what an experience of union is. Sometimes the person suspects that an enlightenment did take place but prefers not to risk exposing it to the light of day and drawing any attention it might draw. Bart was a little shy, and what he experienced wasn't like anything he thought he was looking for:

Bart, aged twenty-nine: *"Can I talk to you about something that happened?"*

Master: *"Yeah, what happened?"*

"Well, two dyads ago I was outside. I was walking around. And I normally have the experience of myself as being mixed up with my body and my personality and my mind and my thoughts. I was walking around like this, as usual, contemplating who I am, and suddenly I had this different experience. I don't think it was a direct experience, but I just experienced a pureness I'd never experienced before . . ."

"Go on."

"Well, I started walking around, and everything looked different. I was seeing things just as they are. In a way it was no big deal. But in another way, I'd never experienced looking at reality this way, just seeing things as they are. And I experienced that I am part of what is."

"Tell me about you."

"Well, I'm me. I'm part of what is."

"Tell me more."

"Well, I'm me. I'm not any of the others [laughing]. I mean, it sounds sort of stupid. But I'm me. I'm not trying to be me, I already am me! Except it's like I'm relating from who I really am for the first time."

"What makes you think this wasn't a direct experience?"

"Well, [smiling] I don't know. It's nothing like what I thought."

"Are you satisfied with this experience of yourself, or do you have some doubt that what you are experiencing is yourself?"

"[smiling] No, it's me all right. [laughter] I'd recognize this guy anywhere now. [laughter] I just . . . I thought I was looking for something else."

"Well, that's how it goes sometimes."

" . . . I feel like that was the first real experience I've ever had in my life, of anything. I feel like, in some way, like I have a new set of eyes. Nothing basic has changed; I just have a new set of eyes."

"Okay, good. Keep presenting yourself to your partners now, okay? Give them the pure you."

"All right, thanks."

It's almost embarrassing to be writing a book about how it is possible to have an actual enlightenment experience in three days. Yet I, and many others, have lived it. In the next chapter are four more accounts of enlightenment experiences.

FOUR ENLIGHTENMENT EXPERIENCES

It is a great mystery.
The Beloved comes at night to the back door
after I have spent the day asleep
and calling loudly from the front lawn.

—Robert Dow

THIS FIRST ACCOUNT is a transcription of an audio cassette-recording made immediately following an Enlightenment Intensive given in Austria in 1984:

1) JOE (AGED FORTY-TWO, AMERICAN)

What happened was that I was going along in the dyads when I suddenly went into union and experienced a nonseparation of everything. I wasn't viewing reality anymore from a separate point, I was in direct union with it. And I began to feel this love for everything. I went for a walk and I felt like kissing the trees. It wasn't the kind of love I'm used to feeling, it was different. It was just this real akin-ness. There's no need to call it love, because it's just that state that really is. I felt like I wanted to start shining everybody's shoes. Just serve them from my heart.

When I look around me now everything is like a roar from God that "I am!" or "See how obvious?!" The beauty of the world is so obvious to me now, so obvious! It's almost continual worship. I feel the essence of a madman somewhere in me. What's going on here in life is so magnificent, compared with how we act like it is. It's practically a crime, how we act in the face of this. If there's any sin, that's it. It's so beautiful as it really is . . . it's just so beautiful.

2) SANDY (AGED THIRTY-NINE, AUSTRALIAN)

On the third day of my first Intensive I directly experienced who I am. It was the most amazing experience I had ever had in my life to that point, and it completely shifted my perspective on everything. I had never really known who I was. I'd always assumed that I was a housewife, or a professional person in the work field, but life seemed very meaningless to me in that situation. Suddenly I had that experience, and I had no idea what was happening to me. I'd never even witnessed anybody else going through that process. I also had all this phenomena happening, like rushes of energy shooting up through my body.

I'd been through various crises leading up to that point, of feeling bad and feeling good, but this was affecting my whole body. I was experiencing my true self, the real me, that I had actually never known existed before. It seemed like a whole, vast universe was opening up. The only way I can describe it was that I was conscious of me, me without any personality, me without any barriers, me without any attachments. I felt like I was on fire, and I just glowed. All I could say was "I'm just me." It sounds strange, sort of too simple, but that's the only way to describe it. I went in being me but not knowing it, and I came out being me, and knowing it. It was this that changed my life. It gave a whole meaning to my life that hadn't been there before. It made my role of being a mother more meaningful than it already was. Before, I just hadn't seen the point in my whole existence. I was being a mother who couldn't figure out what I was here for. This all changed after that Intensive.

3) RUSSELL (AGED THIRTY-TWO, CANADIAN)

The first direct experience I had was working on the question "Who am I?" I experienced the me that I really am. And with this came the clarification for me that I'm not my body or my feelings, or my thoughts or my concepts, or any ideas about how to live that were bequeathed to me from my parents. I'm not even my mind. In fact, that's the greatest thing that I'm not! Also, I realized that even though I'm not those things, I do have those things. I am me-ness that has certain things associated with it, like a mind, a body, feelings, and ideas. I have those things associated with me, but pervading all those things, is me.

What happened just after that experience is that there was this uncontrollable urge to laugh. I thought it was so funny, this realization, so hysterically funny. Because it was so obvious. Yet I had missed it for all of my life, this basic fact that who I am is me. I remember thinking that I am the punchline, that there was this joke that had gone on for the whole of my life, and not only had I realized the punch line, the punch line was me! The joke was that all my life I'd been looking for myself, and looking into so many other areas to find myself, yet I never really looked at the one that was looking. And the one I was looking for was the one who was looking. I just laughed and laughed hysterically over that. And I remember after that, there was this complete feeling of bliss and harmony within myself. Nothing seemed to be an effort, and there was nothing that I wanted to resist.

4) RUSSELL

4) On my next Intensive I worked on "What am I?" And I went through various periods of resistance and emotions and finally emptiness. I had been struggling with the word 'God'. It kept coming up as what I am, and I had been setting it aside, at first because it seemed like just an answer, and I wanted an experience. Later, I set it aside because I didn't want the responsibility. And I was concerned. What would people say, if I was God? Finally I got past all that and there was one dyad, right after rest period on the third day, when my partner said "Tell me what you are" and it was as if for the very first time I heard the question. And in that moment I experienced myself as everything. It was with such clarity that I couldn't deny it. It came into my consciousness, and there was nothing, not even a million people persecuting me and telling me I was wrong, not even that would dissuade me from the knowledge that what I am in my true nature is everything.

Just after that experience I felt this immense bliss and ecstasy. It was painful even, the immensity of realizing that. This experience did not negate in any way my earlier experience of who I am. It actually unfolded or expanded that first experience into what I am. Although I am everything, I can be involved in one thing. I realized the true immensity of myself, and it was extremely freeing.

THE CLOSING TALK
AND
WHAT TO DO AFTER AN ENLIGHTENMENT
INTENSIVE, PART I

BY THE END OF THE ENLIGHTENMENT INTENSIVE, there is no one single way that everybody is. Usually, some are still contemplative, some talkative, and some are a little ecstatic from the contact with others or the breakthroughs they've had. Some may be disappointed that they didn't break through before the end. Some may be in love with the method and want it to go on and on. Some may be just glad it's over. There is usually a group spirit of accomplishment and a sense that something real was undertaken. People often feel much closer to each other.

The closing talk is usually brief. The staff is acknowledged and thanked, practical matters are taken care of, such as who needs a ride home, and then a few final tips are given for re-entering normal life:

Ok, you've done a lot of hard work, and I appreciate the spirit in which you applied yourself to this practice. There are a few things I can recommend now that you do that will help you complete the Intensive for your-self. One is to get some rest tonight. You might be energized and happy to sit up all night talking, but for a better transition I would get some sleep. And remember, when you get home, the people in your life haven't been spending the last three days doing this, so don't expect them to be on the same page with you. Part of your project now as you ease back into your life is to keep this in mind and be considerate of the others in your life who spent the weekend doing other things.

You never know what you're going to get when you take an Enlightenment Intensive, even if you've taken one of these things before. Sometimes it ends and there is a nice sense of completion about what you've done. Sometimes you are in the middle of some god-awful barrier and you haven't broken through. Because we are so different in our processes, this is unavoidable. But the work you have done, whether you broke through to your satisfaction or not, was a good effort and a good practice. Anytime you sincerely apply yourself to a practice like this, it will tend to forward your spiritual evolution and contribute to whatever efforts you make in the future, no matter what method you use.

The main question people usually have after taking an Enlightenment Intensive is, "What should I do now with what I've experienced?" This is a good question, and there are many answers to it. In simple terms, there are three basic approaches I recommend.

The first is to find some people who can relate to what you've experi-enced and include them in your circle of friends. This gives you people in your life with whom you can share at the level of what you've experienced. This in turn helps ground what you've experienced into life.

The second is to try to follow your natural interests, respect your rela-tionships, and tell the truth. This will tend to naturally lead you to where you next need to go, wherever it is.

The third is to make a project out of finding out how experiences of truth are brought into life. Even if you didn't break through into direct experience, you have gone deeper into your process and touched on levels of truth and contact beyond what ordinary life usually has to offer. A lot of books have been written about this project, and seekers in every tradition have had to deal with it in some way or another. It's the next natural project that's there in this work. If you follow up on whatever interest you have in this, it will lead you to more information and practices of different types, and you can see where you want to go next.

Sometimes people have an experience of one kind or another after the Intensive is over, sometimes even an enlightenment experience. If that happens, go ahead and contact me or one of the staff people. If you have questions about your personal process and where to go with it, I'd be happy to talk with you about that too. Okay, that's it. Thank you again for all your work. Let's go and eat those pies over there.

Toronto, 1985, after the Closing Talk. Enlightenment Intensive mastered by Russell Scott.

It's not the time and place right after an Enlightenment Intensive to go into the follow-up project in any depth, it's time to do things like eat pie and relax. But the spiritual problem of bringing important experiences into life is nevertheless there for many people who complete an Enlightenment Intensive. Before going on to the personal accounts ahead, which show how a number of people have dealt with this, it is worth getting a fuller perspective on the issue.

I have had the opportunity over the years to look at what a lot of different people did after taking Enlightenment Intensives. There is great variation, which the personal accounts ahead plainly show. There really is a profound uniqueness to each of us, along with an equally profound commonality that we share. The flowering of this paradox into life is often wondrous to behold. Yet, in specific terms, the Enlightenment Intensive remains silent on what you should or shouldn't do as follow-up practice afterwards. Often the master will recommend this or that out of his or her own experience, as I have done above, but different masters say different things, and the method itself says nothing. This point is sometimes protested. More than once I've heard someone say, "The Enlightenment Intensive is great but it really needs more follow-up practice." This is one of its built-in ironies: a lot of the appeal of the Enlightenment Intensive is that it is not inextricably connected to any system. People go knowing they won't be joining a religion or having to follow some person or program afterwards.

But then many come to feel this lack of ongoing support, which whole religious systems, teachers, spiritual communities, and ongoing practices are meant to provide. Sometimes a finger of blame even gets pointed back at the Enlightenment Intensive, as if it were a harsh teacher, sending people off into the night with a new consciousness but no owner's manual.

There is some validity to this charge. Ideally, Enlightenment Intensives would be one aspect of a comprehensive program for personal growth. But part of the problem here is also a misunderstanding of the full spectrum of spiritual growth and the place of techniques such as the Enlightenment Intensive in it. The Enlightenment Intensive was never meant to be a complete path, only an awakening tool. It is sometimes the source of a rebirth for people, but it does not provide everything for life outside the womb. To expect it to do so is like a new mother complaining to the midwife that her services do not provide instruction for the child in basic speech. "WHAT? YOU'RE NOT GOING TO TEACH HIM HOW TO TALK? YOU'RE GOING TO JUST HAND HIM TO ME LIKE THAT?" Everything goes better when a compassionate midwife is honored for the vital service she provides, no more, no less. In spiritual growth terms, the Enlightenment Intensive holds a similar place. One day a fuller, more complete system may be developed around it, but that has not happened yet. In the meantime, people have sometimes struggled to integrate their experiences into life, a process that appears to be more or less a struggle for anyone experiencing enlightenment, no matter what system was used. The first step in this process is to understand the two main types of spiritual experiences.

TWO TYPES OF SPIRITUAL EXPERIENCES: AWAKENING AND FULFILLING

Someone who has spent years in spiritual practices will look back and identify two general categories of experiences that make a difference. One type is the awakening breakthrough experience that transitions us into a new way of viewing life and relating to others. Enlightenment would certainly be in this category, as well as peak experiences, major insights, getting through a healing crisis, transitional passages such as giving birth, and so on.

The second type is the bringing of the awakenings to earth, the fulfilling of their promise, their direction, their truth. This means letting one's heart, mind, and being transform so that they are a reflection of what has been experienced. For example, it's one thing to be awakened by direct experience into the awareness that one is not the mind. It is another to actually behave that way on a moment-to-moment basis. It is more difficult in practice to no longer believe the mind when it comes up to say things like, "You can't succeed at what you want."

It's one thing to be awakened to the fact that our relationships are fundamentally sacred. It is another to always deal with them that way in practical terms. It's

one thing to realize that one has a special talent and gift to give to the world. It's another to actually give it unreservedly.

Spiritual experiences of the first type, including direct experiences, are normally sudden and more or less surprising. Spiritual experiences of the second type are normally gradual, hacked out over time, sometimes a long time, through regular practice of a technique or the application of simply living more truly to oneself. These experiences are neither sudden nor spectacular and are usually characterized by daily cultivation and the facing of the mundane issues of human life: work, health, family, finances, dealing with especially irritating people, and so on. With the second type, we usually don't realize the progress we've made until we look back one day and notice that we've progressed and that it's stable.

These two categories of spiritual experiences are well known in Zen. Philip Kapleau, in *The Three Pillars of Zen*, quotes the lectures of Zen Master Yasutani Roshi, who said:

> Even after *kensho*, when you perceive that everything is one and are no longer confronted by an external world, you still cannot live in and through that experience. Somehow you keep returning to the previous state of mind. However, if you continue work on subsequent *koans*, each time you resolve another *koan*, that experience is reaffirmed and you return to the world of non-duality with greater clarity. Gradually the clarity and the ability to live in this world of oneness improve.
>
> So there is both suddenness and gradualness in Zen training. The experience of awakening is sudden, but the integration of the experience into your life is gradual.

The point here is not that *koan* work is the only way to deepen spiritual experiences because it isn't. Most spiritual systems have the goal to integrate spiritual experiences and the variation among them of how to go about doing that is vast. The main point here is that in spiritual terms there are two basic projects to consider: awakening and integration.

What is the relationship between these two categories? How do they interact to form the two legs of truth-living? Let's look first at the breakthrough experience. What I have to say applies more or less to any breakthrough experience, whether a deep insight or an enlightenment experience. But let's assume here for the purpose of looking at this that you have been fortunate enough to have directly experienced some aspect of reality on an Enlightenment Intensive.

THE STORY, THE MEMORY, AND YOU

Some minutes, hours, or days after the energy of the enlightenment experience has subsided, what you are typically left with can be loosely categorized into three parts: there's the story of what happened, the memory of the union that was experienced, and the union, or enlightenment, itself.

The story is usually something like: "It was the third day and I was out on a walk. We were in the Sierra Mountains and the air was really clear. I sat down by this tree to contemplate. I was just looking at a stick on the ground and something happened . . ."

In the story there is always a time, a place, a sequence of events, and so on. But enlightenment is not a story. It's a timeless, indescribable actuality. It's you-truth. And although one may become especially fond of the particular place and people associated with the breakthrough, the transformative power of direct experience does not lie in the telling and retelling of the story. It's okay to tell the story. This is usually important to do after it's happened. In some way it's as if the story *wants* to be told, and it can come to have inspirational value. But it's overall value in the long term is usually much less than first thought.

Along with the story there lingers the memory of the awakening. This is not the sequence of events leading up to it but the memory of the new consciousness at the time of the breakthrough. This memory, although a mental facsimile, never-

theless can have more lasting value than the story. It can spur us on to further spiritual enquiry. When we occasionally recall the awakening experience via the memory and compare it with how we are being and relating now, it can give us the real direction to go in. It's like a signpost pointing the way out of neurotic behavior and the hell of the mind. Contemplation of the memory can also serve as a doorway for coming into touch with the reality that one originally experienced, so that one re-experiences it here and now. The memory can be useful in other ways, for example in reading scripture. Scripture, from any time or any place in the world, can hold a deeper fascination than before, because it speaks of something now known to some degree. The memory of enlightenment has more practical uses than the story. But, it is not the pearl.

The pearl is you, the true, awakened you. You are not a story, a memory, not something that happened once, not even something existing in time. There's no thing there, no solid object, no concept, no nothing. But it's real, and it's you, the one reading these lines. We show up by our presentation of who we are, how we live and relate with others. This is a highly individualistic process, shown in more detail by the personal accounts ahead. And this process raises an interesting question: "In an enlightenment experience, what gets transformed?"

WHAT GETS TRANSFORMED?

The question of what gets transformed becomes increasingly perplexing as one consistently sees people directly experiencing their true nature as perfect, yet not any thing; as ultimately indivisible, undiminishable, eternal, and wholly beyond such ideas as "evolution" or "transformation." It just doesn't happen, in any enlightenment method, that a person will come to directly experience the true self as being in some way flawed, crimped, half-baked, or somehow in need of "growth." In fact, the whole idea that the true self might in some way "grow" or "evolve" eventually becomes laughable.

What, then, gets transformed? If we are perfect in our nature before enlightenment, during enlightenment, and afterwards, what changes? It is subjectively clear that something evolved, but what is it, if not me?

What evolves and transforms in the process and nonprocess of enlightenment is the state of our relationship with the way things actually are. Whereas before one was not fully conscious of a certain key aspect of reality (others, for example) one now *is* conscious of it, and can therefore relate with it on a truer, more real basis. Who and what we are do not appear to actually evolve. In the accounts ahead, who and what each person is remained the same throughout their life. What transformed was their consciousness, their awareness of self and others, not in the mental realm of the intellect but at the very source of their being. Thus their ability to live from themselves and recognize who and what others really are, evolved.

TROUBLED GROWTH AND SPIRITUAL GROWTH

This clarifies one of the fundamental differences between the approach to growth that the troubled individual typically takes and the nature of spiritual growth that begins to take place after an awakening. A troubled individual will often suspect that either others are flawed and have to change or *I'm* flawed and have to change. Either underlying assumption will tend to keep a person trapped in cycles of inner strife and dissatisfaction with others. In this condition, life and relating become about sophisticated or blunt forms of manipulation, alternated with coping strategies such as the overuse of drink, food, or drugs. It is not a happy or positive context. It is fundamentally a problematic view of self, life, others, and growth.

Often our journey begins with growth based on a troubled mind, wrong ideas, and some personal problems to be attended to, but enlightenment can graduate us into the realm of spiritual development more consistent with our true nature and that of others. It makes spiritual growth make more sense, even to the formerly atheistic. Relating, living, and spiritual growth become less of a problem and more of an opportunity, a project, an adventure, a divine unfoldment. The personal accounts ahead reveal this particular transition.

THE HOPE OF ONE BIG BREAKTHROUGH

In the early stages of seeking, and because of these underlying assumptions of being themselves flawed, beginners in enlightenment work are sometimes hoping for a big, sudden experience to occur, after which life can be lived effortlessly. They are essentially searching for a cure. Certainly breakthrough experiences are important, but the idea that you have one big one and then everything will be all right is childlike in it's simplicity. It reflects the dissatisfaction felt by the individual, and also the individual's status as a newcomer to spiritual growth. A common corollary to this misguided thinking is the idea that children are enlightened. They do appear so, because of their spontaneity and lack of "mindstuff" as compared to adults, but this is deceptive. We are actually highly dependent as children, weak and fragile, deeply ignorant of the true tests of life ahead. Yes, many holy men and women have said, "We must be as children," but it is a poetic analogy, not a literal one. The childlike qualities of an accomplished spiritual seeker are well balanced by inner power, wisdom, and choiceful surrender, which have been hard-won through the great ups and downs of long-term living and spiritual practice.

THERE IS MORE WORK TO DO

It is one of the ancient, most central teachings that after enlightenment there is work to do to stabilize and fulfill the awakening into one's being, body and life. The stories of the single, final enlightenment, such as that of Buddha, are wonderful stories. But Buddha, it is said, worked hard for nine years in his legendary effort. He certainly would have had many intermediate direct experiences and ongoing struggles to stabilize what he had become conscious of.

In terms of Enlightenment Intensives, what I've seen is that the people who go on with enlightenment work eventually satiate their drive for the truth in terms of breakthrough experiences of it. The "searching" mode undergoes a transformation. One becomes less interested in having breakthrough experiences. They are okay, even wonderful, but are no longer the aim as such. The project to live from and fulfill what has been experienced begins to take precedence. A maturation process takes place.

The irreplaceable advantage of an enlightenment experience is that it clarifies the way to go for a life and a deeper spiritual practice based more in who and what we really are. Often, as a side effect, it blows out some of the resistances to going ahead. It can annihilate pain and the sense of desperation. One may still have neuroses. But the neuroses become counterbalanced now by an inner experience of something wholly beyond neurosis, a truer experience of self, life, and others. It becomes much easier to abandon neuroses because now there is something viable to go toward: a life based on real relating rather than acting out. In the project of the work to do after enlightenment, one may also be internally challenged by an enlightenment experience: "If I am connected to all others by love, then my jealousies and driving competitiveness just aren't going to stand up." If a man directly experiences others as undeniably of the same nature as he, for example, this knowledge makes it harder thereafter to invest much energy in bigotry or hatred.

In Zen practice, the first stage awakenings, something regularly seen on Enlightenment Intensives, are understood to be the beginning of the real process of continued practice, not at all any place to stop. This is why a three-day Enlightenment Intensive is not enough, why any short-term growth method is never enough, why you never see people have one big experience and then have no other trials in life or further spiritual work to do. In fact, from my observation, life's more difficult tests can just as easily come after enlightenment as before.

Spiritual work of the second type, of transforming one's relationship with reality on a daily basis, is a highly personal thing in terms of what forms and practices should be done, if any. In the personal accounts ahead, you will get to know a number of people who have dealt with these two forms of spiritual growth for most of their lives, from the traumas of childhood through the struggle to awaken to the challenges of bringing their gifts to others on a daily basis. They sought, and to one degree or another, they found. Then they actualized, succeeding more and more. The place Enlightenment Intensives holds for them is explained by each within the greater context of their life experience, their propensities, talents, callings, and awakenings. For all these people, the path continues, making the following chapters simply progress reports. But for the reader who can settle down and listen to what each of these individuals has to say, many subtle answers to the question of "What happens after enlightenment, and what is there to do?" may be found.

PERSONAL ACCOUNTS

DAWN:
ENLIGHTENMENT AND THE HEALING POWER OF COMPASSIONATE TOUCH

Dawn Nelson is the founder of COMPASSIONATE TOUCH,™ a program of supportive touch and massage for the elderly, the infirm, and the dying. Dawn developed the program from her background in massage therapy and her experiences on Enlightenment Intensives. What does self-awakening have to do with touch and healing, I wondered, and how did Dawn develop this synthesis? I went to find out. I first interviewed Dawn in 1984 when she was aged forty-one, and, for further perspectives, again in 1995 at age fifty-two.

I had issues from my childhood in Kansas and I began seeking ways to heal them. In 1945, my father was off in the war and one night, when I was thirteen months old, my mother went on a drinking binge and didn't come back. After three days the neighbors called the police about a crying infant in a dark house. And they came and got me and took me to the hospital, and I didn't die. This was all in the newspapers. The courts declared my mother unfit, and my grandparents were given custody of me. So this set up for me a lot of tapes that I'm not good enough to be loved, I'm not pretty enough, or whatever, and it deeply affected my life. I didn't trust people that they wouldn't abandon me, and all that.

In 1978 a friend of mine told me about the Enlightenment Intensive. She said it was the most powerful thing she had ever done. She also said that during it, she reached a place where she faced death, and I remember I got a little scared about that. So I sort of forgot about it for two years. And then one day I decided to take one, and I signed up. Soon after, I began having all these fantasies and expectations about it, from what my friend had said. I got scared. I talked about this with the person I was going to the Intensive with, and she and I agreed that if it got too rough we would give each other a certain sign and then leave.

Well, it didn't turn out anything like that for me. It was a good lesson for me about having expectations. I never wanted to leave, the time passed very quickly, and I was sorry when it was over. What impressed me the most was the focus. To sit opposite another person and for half the time to be listened to without someone evaluating or judging or even having any dialogue about what I was saying, and the other half of the time to be listening and just understanding, that one activity was so powerful for me.

I took several more Intensives in that period. On my third one, I had a direct experience which completely changed how I relate with others. I was working on "What is another?" And at one point I was working with someone I had been avoiding to work with for the whole Intensive. I finally realized that that person is another, and I should face what the fear is. So I went up to this person and asked if we could do the next dyad together. And in the middle of that next dyad, while I was being open in this new way, I directly experienced that person. We became one. There was no difference between us. It's hard to describe this in words. But as soon as I had experienced this, it's as if my body disappeared totally, and there was just this oneness that existed. There was no thought about me being me, and this other person being this other person. We were the same.

The phenomena that went with this was light. I felt like a statue of Buddha or something, and I could feel light coming into the top of my head, and going out of it, and joining with this other person. There was no sense of time; it was as if it lasted for an eternity. Probably it was ten minutes that this light was pouring out of me. And I experienced this love in all of that, that was just there.

That experience changed forever my relationships with other people. It was like having on sunglasses and suddenly taking them off and seeing people for the first time. I had experienced there being no difference between myself and another, and I began to really want to treat people better because of that, not from some teaching but from what I had actually experienced. It totally changed my viewpoint of what another is. I experience so much less separation now between me and others. It made others so much more accessible to me. And it began to transform how I worked as a massage therapist.

Comments on integration from the second interview in 1995:

People who are living out their lives in a health care facility, or are dying at home, can't go out and get a massage. Many can't even ask for it. So my purpose in creating COMPASSIONATE TOUCH™ was to take that kind of nurturing and attention to people who are less mobile or nonverbal. I work with a lot of people who cannot speak, either because of a stroke or a dementia-related condition, or they are so near death, or for other reasons. And touch, being a universal language, is a way of communicating with these people, offering support and nurturing.

My work is growthful, and my practitioners are challenged to look at their own issues about death and dying. They are challenged to confront death, basically. Anybody who is going to enter into close contact with a dying person has to deal with this. Yet I have found that when you get into contact with the individual, when you take your attention off the body and the illness and the fact that the person is dying, then suddenly you're in contact with this individual, and you begin to have this very rewarding experience. Because it's not like, "Oh, you're in this terrible shape and I'm in this great shape," it's more like, "Oh. We are these two individuals. And we are just relating. And you happen to be in a body that's got cancer."

The strength in my work is that I have gained the ability to put my attention on the individual, on who and what the person is, rather than on the disease or the physical condition or a mental state. I can do this because I know that those other things are just those other things, they aren't who the person is. I think that's what people notice about my work and why they are drawn to it when I teach it. The attention given to the elderly and the ill is usually on the disease or the behavior or the fact that death is near, it's not on the person. But individuals respond to the fact that "someone has their attention on me." They respond when they experience, "This person is not trying to fix me or change me or take care of my body, this person is just relating to me." I wouldn't have that ability if I hadn't taken Enlightenment Intensives.

Probably the biggest thing I've gotten from Intensives, in terms of living life, is the ability, not always easy in practice, to let someone be who he or she is. And to realize that things really are a certain way. That profoundly affected my relationship with others, to really get that. And I know that some people can't grasp that concept. I say it to them, and they go "Uh?" And in my past I probably couldn't have gotten it either if someone had just said it to me. I got the ability from doing Enlightenment Intensives, and it's one of the main things I take to my work now. I always speak about this ability. And I do meet people who know exactly what I'm talking about; they just got it from somewhere else, in some other way. And this has helped me drop the idea that you have to take an Enlightenment Intensive in order to get what I'm talking about here. But that's how I got it.

In 1990 I took the first Enlightenment Intensive I had taken in years. At one point I was in a dyad and I started getting something. And this is very hard for me, because I've been so hung up on this point . . . but I got that I am, also, what I see in others. I experienced that what I am is love, truth, and everything I can see in others. I experienced that that's what I am too.

And in that moment I felt my father's presence. He had died about two years before this. And at the same time it seemed as if this golden light of angels filled this huge space of the room. I felt their presence, I saw them in my inner vision, and I heard them singing. And I got that nobody had ever not wanted me to experience what I really am. I experienced that there was all this help and support in the universe, and that other people got who I am, I just hadn't got that fully myself.

This really helped me resolve at a new level the issues of my mother's abandonment of me that happened in 1945. It sort of blew away this idea that I'm not good enough, that I don't deserve good things to happen to me because my mother didn't want me. I just couldn't live out of that idea any more. I still have vestiges of it, but it's not so deep now. I spend my time now mainly being with my family and forwarding COMPASSIONATE TOUCH™, which is well received and which I find extremely rewarding. In terms of Enlightenment Intensives, I still take them sometimes, and I also give them occasionally. They have meant everything to me. They've been so very, very significant. They gave me a vehicle for growth that's more powerful than any other I've found.

PETER:
ENLIGHTENMENT AND THE MARTIAL ARTS

Peter Ralston is a former martial arts World Champion who took Enlightenment Intensives in the early 1970s as part of his inner development, which he cultivated along with his physical training. The fruits of his work in both realms was first seen by the public in 1978 in Taipei, Republic of China, at the World Championship Chinese Martial Arts Tournament. The Chinese, who take their martial arts seriously, made this a full contact event in which contestants fought without protective gear or padded gloves. On their hands they wore only light, unpadded gloves to help the judges see the action. Eight years earlier, a similar tournament had been conducted that resulted in serious injuries, so the rules in this one were that no strikes to the head or groin were permitted. Otherwise, it was wide open. Over 170 contestants from around the world showed a variety of fighting styles, most of them using a form of Kung Fu.

Peter arrived as a complete unknown and showed a mastery of form and sensitivity that took the Asian audience and his opponents by surprise. Fighting in the light-heavyweight division, he won his first match when his Korean opponent-to-be watched him warm up and then declined to enter the ring when the actual bout was to begin. He advanced untouched through the preliminary rounds and won the final handily, becoming the first non-Asian ever to win a tournament of this kind.

Most people who take an Enlightenment Intensive have not achieved world-class proficiency at their discipline, so Peter is certainly atypical in this respect. However, his experience shows the transformative effect that enlightenment can have when there is a solid base of training and discipline into which it can flow.

Here is what he had to say to me in 1979, at age twenty-eight, about a year after winning the World Championship. I also checked in with him again in 1996, to see how things looked to him at that stage. By that time a lot of water had gone under the bridge and he had a number of important comments to make on integrating enlightenment into life:

When I was young, I wanted to be the best fighter in the world. I mastered certain martial art principles, got some black belts, and then I started to understand that if I was really going to be the best, then I would have to become more powerful in a lot more ways than just physical competency. I didn't use the term then, but the real meaning behind what I was after was that it would take a real transformation for me to accomplish that. I mean, I had to change, and I really had to do it. So I began to study Zen and the Tao Te Ching, in order to do this. But, by and by, it all turned around and my martial arts began to further my study of that, of discovering my own true nature.

See, around that time, as a teenager, I would go to classes and fight with black belt karate people and win, but still feel like I lost. I would win and feel bad. Something wasn't right. The thing about it was I was winning from natural ability, because I was stronger, quicker, and more aggressive. But I wasn't winning because I really understood anything about martial arts or personal transformation. It was just a relative thing. Somebody who was faster and stronger than me would have beaten me. It wasn't right.

So I began to study the softer forms of martial arts: Tai Chi and Kung Fu and others. I continued to train a lot and be fairly isolated. Then one day when I was twenty-one, a friend of mine named Mark Ederer told me he really wanted me to do something called an Enlightenment Intensive. He described it, and I just couldn't see how anything significant could be brought about in only three days of intensive contemplation. I thought, "Enlightenment? That takes thirty years! And you have to be in a cave!"

But finally I took one in Santa Rosa. I didn't have a direct experience on that first one, but by the end of it, I felt more joy than I had ever felt in my life. I was really happy. I realized that I hadn't even noticed before that I hadn't been happy. So, from this, I was sold on Enlightenment Intensives.

Two weeks later, I went up to a place called Origin in the Sierra mountains and did my second one, this time working on "What am I?" I spent the entire time very willfully and very dynamically going for a direct experience of what I am. I threw everything I had into it for three days, solid, every moment. I didn't let up, at least I didn't notice that I did. And I didn't get it. I didn't directly experience what I am. But the next day, in the late afternoon, I was sitting against a wall and I suddenly had a major breakthrough, the nature of which was completely outside of all my previous experience. It was somehow outside of 'experience' and, at the same time, it completely transformed my experience.

I was suddenly aware that I was nothing, absolutely no thing. I directly experienced my true nature not as thingness in any way, shape, or form. The possibility that I wasn't anything had not existed for me in my contemplation. In the enlightenment I was just . . . no thing, no where, no substance whatsoever. Yet it was me.

After this, abilities like being able to read somebody's disposition accurately started to come. In fighting, I was able to see what people were going to do before they did it. So, when somebody was going to hit me, I would finish the situation before they were able to, and that was it. I was just dealing with the situation in a more real way. I was dealing with what was true.

Sometime later I did a two-week Enlightenment Intensive. The whole two weeks was tough sometimes, I'll tell you, but it was very powerful. I worked on "What is life?" I was in the very last dyad of the whole two weeks, and to make a long story short I thought if I hadn't gotten it in fourteen days, what difference could this last dyad make? I was just enjoying myself, sort of playing around. Then, while I was in this kind of play, I suddenly had an experience of what the Zen people call "the void." I experienced that absolute existence doesn't exist. There was no distance, no space, no time . . . nothing.

I recognize now that I didn't have a context in which to hold that experience. I had experienced the absolute nature of existence, yet when I was back in life all I noticed in practical terms is that everybody lied. Everything said and everything done was a lie. It was not the absolute truth. And it started to become intolerable. Then I noticed that everything I said was a lie, that I wasn't able to speak the absolute truth. I didn't know what to do with it. From this, I think it is invaluable to have a context in which to hold such an enlightenment experience.

In martial arts, new abilities started to arise. Previously, I was able to read someone before they moved. I could perceive the origin of the action. Now I didn't have to be cognizant of any movement on their part, psychic or otherwise, to know what to do. I didn't have to perceive a thing. The other ability was perceiving the beginning. But with this, I wasn't perceiving anything. I just knew. And that blew me away.

I found that in fighting I would start to move, and then my opponent would throw a kick or a punch, and I saw that I was moving out of the way of their action, but I was doing it before I even knew why! I'd just move, and they would throw a kick and miss. And I'd think, "If I'm moving before I know what he's going to do, how do I know if he's going to move this way or that? What if I move and it's not appropriate?" Then I started to notice that I kept doing it appropriately.

So I knew some time before I did the World Championship that my playing the game of learning martial arts and mastering it was coming to a close. In 1975 I went and looked at masters and teachers all over Asia, and there was nobody I wanted to study with. So I had in one sense given up martial arts before I even did the World Championship. But I did the World Championship for a couple of reasons. I wanted to complete something for myself and begin something new. The completion part was that I was no longer going to be involved in that part of martial arts, the getting better and competing. I also wanted some recognition. I'm quite different in the world of martial arts. I ask people to do uncommon things, to take on apparently unrelated enquiries, and I demand a very deep level of understanding. And I want people to listen to me, to open up to what I'm saying. So winning the World Championship was done so I could say, "I did it. What I'm teaching you is functional. It works." Now, people are more likely to consider what I'm saying, even though I'm saying the same things as before.

One thing I also started to notice was that my understanding in martial arts and other things that I do in my pursuit . . . see, I don't like calling it "martial arts" any more because it's so much more than that . . . but my understanding was not being reflected in the rest of my life to the degree it was in my work. So, I started to change that around, to look at that, and approach things differently. It's been difficult. When I stopped isolating myself, it was a whole other kettle of fish. I found that to deal with one's entire relationship to life is the most demanding endeavor. Yet I discovered that the things that come up between people— events and so-called problems—are really parallel to what occurs in martial interaction and in fighting. However, translation from one domain to the next is not easy. It requires a fundamental experience of the principles involved, such that they can be recognized in any form. And it also requires a training ground, the purpose of which is to transform the very body and being of the individual into alignment with those principles.

One of the difficult things for people to accept in all this is that violence is an aspect of the world. It is not something which is apart from truth. I've seen people who view 'truth' as something which is apart from the very raw quality of the world. Like truth is only light and love and floating around. And I don't choose to look at it in that way. What I consider to be the truth is the truth. Avoiding the shitty, bad, violent, cruel things, or that which we label as such, is not to be with the world, is not to really turn to the truth of it. And to avoid it is not to transcend it.

The enlightenment experiences that I had helped me immensely in this. Most people haven't had a direct experience of their true nature and can't readily lock onto that truth. But that experience is largely responsible for my being able to detach myself from a point of view. It was knowing what I am that enabled me to see situations more clearly, so I could just give up my point of view, my demand.

Enlightenment Intensives are very pure, and very powerful, and the benefit they had for me I can't say enough about. I recommend them to martial art students, and to any-one, really. I've incorporated the method into my own training of students. But I don't see enlightenment as the end. People with a spiritual gig going often look at it that way. There are stories of complete enlightenment finally reached, Gautama Buddha and all that. But holding it like that is not functional for our purposes. If an enlightenment experience is complete, then it is complete in every way that you can think of it. Every facet and dimension is complete. What I see happens is that somebody has an enlightenment expe-rience, and it is absolute, but not complete. To the degree that it is not complete, it leaves you with the struggle of incorporating it into your life.

Reflections on the integration of enlightenment, 1996:

I had a completely unexpected experience a couple of years ago on one of our Intensives. It was that I can't die. And what was weird about it is that you could have asked me any time before that, "Can your true nature die?" and I would've said, "No, it's not alive, there's nothing there," and so on. But in this experience, what I got is that I can't die! It wasn't like, "My absolute true nature can't die," it was "I can't die." My true nature is not something other than me.

About bringing enlightenment experiences into life, my experience now is that you can't do it. They don't fit. It's also my experience that you can bring them into life, because they're already there. When we start thinking that "first you have a direct experience and then there is some thing to bring into life" then we are off base already. That way of thinking traps us. And one of the things I've gotten since our last conversation, which was, when, 1979? is that I really appreciate paradox more. I can let paradox be a standard now. For example, enlightenment experiences don't fit into life. And they do.

One of the things I remember expressing in 1979 is that I had no way to speak, I hadn't created a language for any of this, and I hadn't created an organization around it. Since then I did that. I've spent the last seventeen years creating ways to communicate this, creating workshops, courses, writing books, and so on. You see, originally, people weren't my concern. My concern was training in the martial arts and contemplating. So it was a real turning point for me around the time of the World Championship, because I made people my business. My endeavor became "how do I communicate to people?"

So I created all sorts of things out of that, the Mind Course, some very powerful workshops, taking on apprentices, dialoguing with people and creating new words and whole systems of thought. I've come to a place at this point where I feel very good now about the relationship between the work I do that is not set on direct experience and the work I do that is set on direct experience. And of course there is an argument that they are the same work. But what I mean is that on the one hand there is the work to do on mind, emotion, thought, relationship, attachment, and ontology (the study of being). There are questions like, what is interaction? What is mind? What is being alive? What is being effective? What is skill? These are questions I pursued for a long time. All of this is a huge domain which does not seem to have an end. It keeps unfolding as you look into it. You get clear on something and then there's more. I suspect there is no end to that part of the process, I suspect it is infinite in nature.

None of that is direct experience. And I don't think there should be any war between the work to have a direct experience and the work in mind and perceptions and relations and all that. They are not the same pursuit. They may ultimately be the same thing, but they are not the same pursuit, and this is where the paradox comes in. I've come to be more at peace with the truth that basically, when you are talking about an absolute, you're never talking about some thing, so you are always living with a paradox. When you try to discuss an absolute, it's always either or neither or both. You can't pin it down. So it's not something you should try to pin down. I'm at peace with that now.

I was just listening to some old Mind Course tapes that somebody sent me, of me talking. And I'm talking along about this and that, and then some guy asks me what a direct experience is. And there's this big pause on the tape [laughter]. That question shuts me off the fastest. There's just no answer. But people want to know. They ask, "What is it? You talk about this thing and it's like up there on a pedestal. Am I pursuing a phantom, or what?" And I pause, because I have no answer, and then I usually say, "Well, I appreciate your angst and your challenge with it, and I'd love to be able to say something without fucking around about it, and I'll try, but I always fall short. There's nothing I can say that will match what a direct experience is." This used to create a pain in my body and my heart. My mind kept trying to tackle it and find something useful to say about it. And I sometimes say useful things about it, but it's not direct experience.

What I'm comfortable with now that I wasn't back in '79 is this challenge to work with people in that paradox. This challenge that we can dialogue and train and work and at some point you will have a direct experience and know what it is or you won't. In the meantime, we'll keep at it. What I say is, "We need to work from the inside and from the outside." And as we keep at it, when it's time to pursue direct experience, which is working from the inside, that's all we should do. And that's what Enlightenment Intensives are all about. They are just for that pursuit, and nothing else. And I don't think they should be fucked with, or have anything added to them. I don't think there's going to be anything that improves the method, basically. Because I think the pursuit of enlightenment should be pure, that when you're doing that, do only that, and nothing else, because that's where the power is. And Enlightenment Intensives are set up for that purity of purpose. There's no hanky-panky. You just suffer through the shit you got to suffer through, and you either have a direct experience or you don't. But if the master starts to supply some answers or say something like, "Now let's mix it with a little yoga and maybe that will help . . ." then no, it won't help. It can't. There is direct experience, and there is the rest. And the rest is the rest. And I think that should be clear. And on that basis, when you work on enlightenment, work only on enlightenment.

EDRID:
SELF-REALIZATION OF A COMPUTER ENGINEER

Edrid is a freelance computer engineer who has lived for many years in the Silicon Valley, south of San Francisco. So far, he has been present at two inspired breakthrough of his times. In 1968 he participated in the first Enlightenment Intensive ever given, and in 1980 he was hired by Steve Jobs at Apple Computer, Inc., to be part of the engineering team that a year later produced the Macintosh computer, an event that transformed how people use information throughout the world. In 1988, he remembered the first Enlightenment Intensive ever given and reflected on where his spiritual development has led him:

I remember on that first Enlightenment Intensive out in the desert, I worked on "What is my true nature?" first. During the initial interview, when Charles assigned the questions, he asked me, "Do you know who you are?" I said, "Well, I know I'm me. I'm this one, here." and I presented it very clearly. It wasn't just my words that convinced him, it was the fact that I did know who I am. He said, "Okay, what do you want to work on?" I said, "Well, I don't really know all of my dimensions. I don't know how I exist, how I come into existence. I don't know enough about myself to be really satisfied with that." It was perfect, because he thought that I should just work on the next question, which was exactly right. So he gave me the choice of questions, "What am I?" or "Tell me your true nature." I decided to try "my true nature."

I had a direct experience on that question on the third day that broke me down. I was crying and experiencing a tremendous sense of relief. Something resolved in me that changed my relationships with everyone from then on. Essentially, I realized how to have a real relationship with everybody. I understood what that was, to have an authentic, real relationship with everyone, and that it was possible. It was a really beautiful experience.

It was a very inspired Intensive. There were several pure "who am I?" experiences, and several others more of the type I had. The physical situation was horrible but we didn't care. We had all heard the Zen stories of how you have to sacrifice in order to get enlightened, and we just got into it.

There was an amazing electric quality to Enlightenment Intensives then that nowadays I don't feel so much. I see people who are just getting into them feel it, but now, for me, it's kind of an old process. It works, it's solid, you can count on it making powerful changes in people's lives. But at the time of the first ones it was all so new, so undiagnosed, so exciting.

On another, later Intensive, I had the biggest self-enlightenment of that period. I had taken my glasses off, because it had been recommended, and I was working with a lady who was like a big earth mother. And she kept saying things that really hooked into my brain. I remember looking at her with my blurry vision, because I normally wear glasses, and suddenly she went crystal clear. I was really taken aback. I thought, "How is this possible?" I looked right next to her, where there was a wood beam, and it was still fuzzy. And this confused me and took me off my question. Right after that the bell rang to end the period and it was time for walking contemplation. I walked out still thinking, "What's going on here? What is my true nature?" I remember looking way down the path where people were still walking, and I looked at them closely, and suddenly they became crystal clear. Apparently there was the right kind of openness because right then it felt like the universe was held off about a foot away, and then the whole weight of it went POW! onto me. It knocked me right on my butt in the dirt.

It was like the heavens opened up. I was filled with an emotion as if a choir of angels had burst out into song. I didn't actually see that, I just felt that way. And I burst out crying and cried for about a half an hour, just lying in the dirt. I was literally swept away by this kind of purging that was going on. I was in a radically different state of consciousness than I was before. I had difficulty characterizing it. And at the end of the period I went down to the interview room and Charles began asking me questions: "What color are you? How big are you? What is your true nature?" And to everything he was asking I was saying, "It doesn't apply. All these things you're talking about aren't what an individual is about. There is nothing at all that an individual is."

That experience really changed my life. The main thing that happened was that the sense of needing to know more about myself pretty much vanished. The other thing is that I was much more simply here, just doing life, rather than having a lot of distance between me and life. I was more in life, more at one with it, after that.

ON INTEGRATION

Enlightenment Intensives have fundamentally changed my relationships. One thing that's really obvious is that if you just live, then after twenty years you'll be at a certain point. You'll grow in certain areas, you'll fail at certain areas. But if in the meanwhile you are doing something like Enlightenment Intensives and spiritual practices, not just philosophizing and talking but doing sincere spiritual practices, then after twenty years you'll be remarkably different than the person who hasn't done that, who hasn't made that investment in their own awareness, in getting rid of subconscious barriers and false ideas about people, and becoming more open.

After twenty years, which is how long I've been doing this, I've gone off on a different track compared to the average person. And I'm absolutely different than I would have been. I just think it would be sad to not experience the truth of the way life really is, ever, in your whole life. It seems like such a sad thing to have been born into life, to live out life and then die, and to never have gotten to the depth of your own being, and the depth of reality, to never have challenged your own awareness, and gone as deep as you can, at least once.

For myself, early on, I was going in the totally wrong direction. I was viewing things purely in an intellectual, superficial way. In high school I was known as the "the Brain," but I was really completely ignorant in terms of consciously experiencing much of anything about life or my true nature. I was really heading in that direction of the realm of intellectual thought, which would have trapped me for my whole life, if it hadn't been for Enlightenment Intensives and the spiritual directions I took. Now, from the time I wake up until the time I go to bed, it's constant in my life, that I live in a certain way, based on the spiritual experiences I've had on Intensives and in other practices I've done. Now, I'm doing life 100 percent, and before I wasn't doing life at all, really, I was just doing intellectual reality.

Over the years I have done a lot of working out of how to really be with people beyond confrontation, and gradually my personal life and my spiritual life have come together. There is no separation now. My religion, my enlightenment became integrated. I feel connected with every individual in the universe. I am in touch with God, all the time, not as a belief but as an experience. And I know that everybody is here all the time. I have no loneliness. That whole process, to get to that point, was over many Enlightenment Intensives, a lot of work with other approaches, and there was no one experience that did it. What happened was that deep roots into truth got put down for me in the

Enlightenment Intensives, and a lot of work came later. And now, I don't have to go into a state or try to remember my spiritual experiences, or think about a theory. The fact that you are divine is not a theory to me, it is a reality, in each moment. That integration pretty much completed around five years ago.

For Enlightenment Intensives to really come into their own, I think they still have to come into the context of a religion or a philosophy that has deeply evolved, creative people in leadership roles, establishing a tradition that will support it. Right now, Enlightenment Intensives are like a body with the head cut off, or a head with no body. It's this incredible technique just sort of floating, waiting for it to be grounded in something that would really support it and round it out and give it dimensions. This is how I see it now.

NANNA:
PSYCHOLOGY, SPIRITUALITY, AND
"THE TWO WINGS OF ONE BIRD"

Nanna is a German psychologist living in Munich. She follows a Tibetan Buddhist spiritual tradition and gives several Enlightenment Intensives a year. Nanna's awakening completely transformed her view of psychology and of what help is. I interviewed her in 1995 when she was aged fifty-four.

In 1983 I took my first Enlightenment Intensive in Munich. I didn't have a direct experience, but I saw someone else have one and by the time the Intensive was over I absolutely wanted to do another. As I took more, though, and didn't break through, I gradually developed doubt about whether I was advanced enough to succeed with them. This doubt went on for several Intensives. But eventually I did break through.

During the Enlightenment Masters Training Course in 1982, I had a direct experience of union with another. It was as if I dissolved and then experienced that another's nature is the same as mine. That we are the same. It was like disappearing into a black hole, and coming out being the other. I became conscious that there is no separated me . . . that I am a reflection of otherness. Everything melted away into emptiness, in a way . . . it was like the contact with the other was the door, and through the door was emptiness, just a void, yet it was another, and it was me, all the same. It was like falling into an eternity.

That was the first important experience I had on Enlightenment Intensives. But before going into how it affected my life, I have to include something that happened on another Enlightenment Intensive some time later. What happened was I directly experienced my father. It seemed to me for all my life that he had been the source of my injuries. And in this experience I experienced him as light, and as perfect. I experienced that by resisting him I had really missed out on the contact with him. And I saw that this was our task in life, to make contact, and yet I had done everything to resist it with him. I had built up my identity to resist him. I understood how I had indeed been injured and how my resistance also caused injury. I saw the whole thing, but I saw also that injury is an illusion in the ultimate sense. I saw that in the absolute realm, there is no such thing as injury; it's all a total illusion. That in the absolute level of reality, no one is ever hurt. All these things I thought my father did to me . . . they just became . . . nothing. All there was was the perfection of him. And the total absence of anything you could possibly call "injury."

By this opening, this giving up my resistance and just receiving . . . him . . . everything I had ever built up and invested myself in, everything I had cherished, my sense of having been wronged and misused and all that . . . which in fact, relatively speaking, was all true . . . all of this dissolved totally. It was difficult, because I saw I had betrayed myself by doing all this drama all these years, by constructing my character around resisting my father. Now it all seemed like just a made-up thing. It seemed just like a game, the game of resisting and drama, that we all play.

I learned from these experiences that there really are two levels of reality: the absolute level and the relative. And that it is not possible to just go directly to the absolute . . . the Buddhists say these two levels are like the two wings of one bird, they must go together. But I didn't know what to do with this at the time.

After these experiences, as a psychotherapist, I began to ask myself "What is help, really?" I grew insecure for a period, not knowing in what direction to help people. I just didn't know what to do. I kept being aware that no one has ever been hurt, in any ultimate way. I kept thinking: what is the job really, in helping people? These experiences destroyed my whole concept of what I was doing in therapy with people, trying to help them with their problems and repair their hurts. I had built my whole career on helping people repair things, and it seemed all useless in that period. In my psychology studies there had been no training in how to deal with experiences like I was having, either in myself or in others

This was one of those experiences in which I felt somehow that I've opened the egg shell but I'm not completely out yet, I'm hanging in it. Yes, I went on, and I continued to help people, but gradually what happened is that I became cured of being the helper, the fixer. I still helped people, but from a different place. It was from a place of understanding that we are going through hurts and dramas and games, but this is not the essential thing we are doing. Before, I thought it was. Now I realized it wasn't. I actually thought it was my job to save people and fix them. I have a broader consciousness about that now. I still get caught in dramas sometimes, but I had really de-identified from the drama of life, and the idea that my life is about fixing the drama of life for people. I had really de-identified from the assumption that we are all playing the hiding game in life, as a drama. That was all gone. And I even started to find the humor in that. And gradually I began to see that I am still useful in helping people, but in a completely different way than before. I no longer think, "I am doing this, and I am doing that, and I am fixing them now." The help now occurs in my contact and work with people, more now actually, than ever, but it is from this more surrendered place of having experienced our true nature.

On one Enlightenment Intensive I experienced myself as being the universe touching itself, through me. It was a clear, simple experience of God . . . of the everything, and me being a part of that . . . there was this incredible beauty, and deep sense of being home. I saw that however far I travel, I can never be away from the center of God. That I can never go so far as to not be in the center of God, of everything. There is no way out! I became very happy about that. I still am.

If I would have an influence, I would include Enlightenment Intensives in the studies that psychologists do. I have seen the method help a lot of people de-identify from roles, from having to be a good "this" or a bad "that," from having to be any certain way, and to begin coming out into life as who they really are. This is an enormous relief for people when this happens.

I especially like it when people have a pure "who am I?" experience. This helps so much when they go into the godly realms later on. I've noticed that people who keep going into the godly realms, if they haven't had this pure experience, they have more difficulty with their surroundings, they get a little egotistical about having experienced these things, and then they need to go through the process of being brought down from that. But if they have the simple "who am I?" experience, then they can just be here for themselves more.

Enlightenment Intensives take people into the world beyond survival. And people start to get really interested in expressing themselves and living beyond mere survival. They often really get how great it is that others exist, that they simply are. And this changes people's lives at the core. People cannot prevent enjoying it and loving this fact. I always like it when people really get that no one is better. And I enjoy seeing people open up to their own rhythms more, their own truth. This is so marvelous, so helpful.

EDDA:
HEALING RACISM

Edda is a Bilingual Education Consultant in California. Ancient writings on enlightenment don't normally address issues of immigration and race, but for many of today's people they are significant barriers to overcome, both in seeking enlightenment and living it. I interviewed Edda in 1995.

I was born in San Juan, Puerto Rico, and each of my grandparents was a different color. I have African, Spanish, and Taino in me. The Tainos were the natives of the island before the Spaniards came.

"When I came to California, I was seven years old, and I immediately picked up on the racism all around me. My cousin used to say, "This is a very racist place. The whites don't like the blacks, the blacks don't like the whites, and the Latinos are in the middle. So don't hang out with the blacks and don't hang out with the whites. And the Latinos aren't going anywhere either, so just keep it cool and stay at home." I resented having Spanish as my native language, I resented being brown in color, and I resented having African features.

This mentality was with me and around me all the time, every day, moment to moment. Even when I was home, my father and my cousin would talk continually about how racist the whole place was. In school I picked up that I wasn't supposed to speak Spanish. The teachers got mad if I did. I just got that being Puerto Rican was definitely not the thing to be. No way. And the only other way to be that was acceptable was to be white. So I thought, "Okay, Edda, the way to make it here is to do the white thing. Learn the language, be it, do it." So I set out to become white. But this got complicated because English didn't come close to allowing me to express myself, to express what's in my heart, the way Spanish does. My real passion shows up in Spanish, but it doesn't in English. So I just put a ceiling on my passion when I switched to English.

This whole dilemma went on constantly for me. Throughout it all I had a hunger inside of me to know who I really am, to really come to terms with that. I continued with my career as a bilingual educator, and then in 1980 a woman came to my house to give me advice about interior decorating. When she walked in, she was one of the most peaceful individuals I had ever come in contact with. And I asked her, "What kind of work have you done with yourself, that makes you so peaceful?" And she said, "I've just done an Enlightenment Intensive." So I said, "Tell me about it." She did, and I said, "Tell me where to call for this."

So I took my first Intensive and I loved it. I really liked sitting with someone and being listened to without interruption. I got really immersed in this question, "Who am I?" and I was fascinated by it. The more I spoke, the quieter I got, inside. I remember being so taken care of by the staff on those three days. And I remember my relationship with food changed. It was so good to just sit and eat simple, good food, in peace, being quiet inside. And on the walks there was this crispness to nature I was seeing that I'd never seen before. All of these experiences were so good for me.

I remember at some time on the second day, sitting by a swimming pool. One of the monitors came up to me, a tall man named Jared. I looked at him and it was like he suddenly disappeared. I saw that his body wasn't what he really is. I somehow saw him, what he really is, and, separately, I saw that he had taken on a body. And I noticed that he didn't have to do that. He took it on out of his choice. I saw that all these identities that Jared had taken on, being male, being tall, being in a body, and all that, he just did that so he could do it. He wasn't doing it because he had to. He did it because that's what you do if you're going to exist in the physical universe. You're going to take on a body and an identity, and then go around in them. From glimpsing him in this way, I saw physicalness showing up out of nothing, out of the nothing that is what we are. Through some miracle, we show up in matter. I'll always remember that flash.

From this experience, and from the whole Intensive, I quieted down inside. When I left, all of that inner turmoil that I had had for the last twenty years of my life, that I had been going to sleep with every night and waking up with every morning, all the terror and stiffness and fear—it was all gone. I woke up in the morning after the Intensive feeling like a normal person for the first time since I was ten. This lasted for more than a week, and parts of all that pain never came back at all.

I did a two-week Intensive after that, had many experiences of different kinds, and afterwards I was in sheer quiet. I went days not hearing any internal chatter or struggle at all. My whole body was different, more pure, at a cellular level. I had this amazing clarity, and I could be with other people, without having any Puerto Rican-ness or blackness or whiteness hanging me up. Nothing, just me. Just me, and you, and that's it. Everything was down to just who you are and who I am, period.

INTEGRATION

Eventually my mind came back, and fear, and anxiety, but nowhere near to the depth it was there before. I still had turmoil, but it was different. It was a longing for God. I truly wanted to know God now, in my heart of hearts, because of the richness I had experienced in the Intensive. I knew it was possible. I wanted to sustain this level of love that I had experienced in the Intensive, this unconditional love, I wanted it in my life, I wanted it in my cellular structure. I came to trust that an Enlightenment Intensive could provide that by the way it is set up. It was a place I could be, without any trips about religion, or anyone trying *to force me to be black or white or brown or anything. I didn't have to be any of that, I could just be who I am. And what I found out that I am, underneath all that stuff, is unconditional love. And it feels like my home, my house, what I've been looking for my whole life. It took away my terror, and my darkness, which I had come to live in, and which I came to know better than I knew my own friends. I found this light of who I really am, and who you are, and the love there really is between us.*

Now, at work especially, there are so many others I come into contact with, people throughout the entire state of California, Spanish-speaking and English-speaking, from the Mexican border to the Oregon border. And most of them don't know who they are. Many are caught up deeply in racism issues. It was hard for me sometimes to go from a state of bliss and clarity after an Intensive and return to work in this death camp of a bureaucracy that I work in. I even pulled out of education at one point because of this. I was restless, from what I had experienced and come to know about life and us. But later I realized that education is my profession, that's where I should be, so I returned, and I came to terms with it. Now I make my way along, not compromising on who I am, and being more able now to see who people are, through all the muck of the bureaucracy. And that's why I'm happy at work now. I can have joy and even bliss sometimes with whoever is in my office, or whoever has a complaint on the telephone, just by relating to who they are. This has permeated my whole life.

And I get to be myself now, rather than white America. And I'm not against white America. It's not a racial thing at all. It's a recovery of me and my passion. And I bring this into my work. Like Gandhi said, "Little by little, in a silent way, you can shake the world." So little by little, conversation by conversation, I talk to the individual. And because I come more from who I am, people get in touch more with who they are, and that's what matters, whether they are black, white, brown, or whatever. This is what keeps me alive in the school system, nothing else.

I usually take one Enlightenment Intensive a year now. I drink of the love and the truth that I find on them. It's like the poet Rumi says: "Wine is being passed, not contained in cups."

JAIME:
SPIRITUAL AWAKENING OF A MEDICAL SCIENTIST, WITH NO CLASSICAL BREAKTHROUGH EXPERIENCE

Jaime's account is important because he has struggled with issues common to some Enlightenment Intensive participants, who work hard and don't have an experience of breaking through. Jaime is a medical scientist and an inventor of diagnostic instruments. He holds a bachelor's and master's degree in electronics engineering, a master's degree in human physiology, a master's degree in business, and a Ph.D. in biomedical engineering. I spoke with him in 1995 when he was fort-eight years old.

The discovery of my spiritual essence has been a gradual thing over the years for me. In each Enlightenment Intensive I have taken, and I have taken around fifteen, I discover a little bit more of the truth. This has happened even though I haven't had one of these full-fledged enlightenment experiences. But I come out of every Intensive with very tangible, very strong pieces of truth that I can incorporate into my life.

My life began changing from the first one. The first thing I discovered was that I'm not really this thinking machine. Later, on another Intensive, I discovered that I'm not my body either. To me, especially as a medical scientist, these have been groundbreaking discoveries.

But I used to worry about not having a direct experience, on the first five or six Intensives I took. The way the process was described, and geared, was all toward getting that experience. But the descriptions didn't match my experience. I just get a chunk of the truth on every Enlightenment Intensive I take, that's how it goes for me. And eventually I lost interest in enlightenment or the enlightenment experience that people were talking about. It's really not a big deal to me to have one of those or not, because what I get for myself is so good that I'm very happy with it. But the first few Intensives, I was so caught up in getting that thing, this enlightenment experience, that I was leaving the Intensive with a sense of loss and of failure, even though I was getting all these clarities and insights about me and life and others. I even went through a period when I resented the way Intensives were being presented. The masters would always say, "Remember, you're going for this enlightenment experience so keep working for that." And, 'It can happen in the last minute, so keep at it!', and so on. Boy. It seemed to me almost materialistic, this idea of "you are going to get something, a real goodie, and you should go for that." When I didn't get it, I would get caught in this idea of somehow being less, of having something wrong with me. I was more or less caught in this trip for many Intensives. And I know people who tried one or two Intensives and didn't have an enlightenment experience, and they didn't come back any more, because they felt they had failed.

I eventually managed to just focus on what I was getting and over time I began to feel that I didn't care about enlightenment experiences. I was still having remarkable experiences, even though they didn't match what I was hearing described as enlightenment experiences.

Enlightenment Intensives have been so different for me than every other part of life, especially being from my scientific background. Science is a very narrow-minded approach to knowing. It's useful for some things. I used to design cardiac pacemakers, and you have to be very single-minded and very focused to do that. But when you are talking about spirituality and truth, you are talking about something much bigger. Science tends to get you thinking. And what I've found now is that my best ideas come when I'm not thinking, when I'm in the shower or something. But most scientists are not much aware of this; they rely almost exclusively on thinking. My ability to stop thinking is something I attribute to the Enlightenment Intensive. I can just detach from my thinking machine and stay in an open space now, when I'm doing my research. But I have a lot of friends who are scientists and engineers, and they don't know what I'm talking about when I try to explain this.

There is something I have learned from Intensives that has been very valuable for me, that I appreciate very much, and I don't know if I can explain it, but I'll try. I have learned that we are all connected to the universe. We are in a flow of energy, an integrated whole. Everything is connected. And when I look at things that way, I approach science completely differently than I did before.

An example is this machine I am working on now that measures blood glucose without taking blood samples, that measures it by using vision and what we know about the retina. I came up with that idea through having a sense of the retina, the eye, myself and our sugar level, all of them, flowing in a connected way. And I thought, "Well, through what would I like to measure the glucose? Well, the eye is pleasant, and we know the retina changes as the glucose levels change, so let's look there."

Normally, diabetics now have to prick their finger several times a day with a needle and get a drop of blood and put it on a piece of litmus paper that costs two cents to actually make, but they are charged one dollar a piece. So there is pain with the pricking, every single day, and it costs $1,000 a year for the paper. And I think about the human being who has to deal with this, on top of being diabetic, and I think about their feelings and their needs. And so I began to wonder, "If I approach the retina the right way, maybe it will tell me how I can measure glucose in a noninvasive way, a way that doesn't involve drawing blood." And it's been doing that, it's been telling me. I have a working system now. I'm at the end of $100,000 grant I received to develop it, and it's going forward into the next phase of development.

My experience is that scientists often see the human being and the body as a machine, as this collection of parts that are each fundamentally separate. I actually got into science because I was curious about how humans work at the source. But I was looking in the wrong places, I was looking for the source of me in the brain, the heart, in the cells, or in the way the cells communicate to each other, and all these things. And I gradually developed a hunch that the source of us is not in any of those places at all. And that's when I began taking Enlightenment Intensives and looking elsewhere. Now I know that if we ignore that spiritual essence within us, which is the source of life, we are wasting our time. A lot of science wastes time looking for the soul in all these mechanisms of the body. I can guarantee them that the soul is not there, but still they look.

Another area of change I've seen in myself as a result of Enlightenment Intensives is in the way I relate to people. I remember one Intensive, I came out feeling that I had discovered people [laughter]. It was that simple. It was like, "My goodness, there are people in the world! And they are like me! And they are exciting and interesting and fascinating!" Boy, that transformed me. I had viewed people before as cardboard, as two-dimensional pictures, I swear, it's almost embarrassing to say it. To me, people were just sort of figures, without too much depth, just figures crossing my landscape. It was a very lonely landscape too. But then I discovered people, and their depth. And this is one of the most intriguing and rewarding things I've gotten from Enlightenment Intensives: how I can see the depth in people now, I see their souls, and I can feel our connection. I have an appreciation for people now, and for relating, that I never had before. I love people now, is really the only way I can say it.

Now I do Intensives the way some people go to church. For me it is a religious, spiritual practice. I think this is what a religion should be about, to put people in touch with their soul, to get people to lead more satisfying lives, to be more in touch with the value of others and the plan of God. I think the Enlightenment Intensive is a very quiet and very powerful religion, and a beautiful process. I haven't found anything that gets close to it. It's intense, it's nondistracting, yet it respects our self-determination and the wisdom that is within us. And I think that's why it's so effective. You feel safe, and so you can be honest and let go and just go for it.

KATHRYN:
EXPERIENCES WITH CHRISTIAN IMAGERY, AND "GOD POURING GOD INTO GOD."

Kathryn holds a Ph.D. in counseling psychology and is an Assistant Professor of Transpersonal Psychology at John F. Kennedy University, in Orinda, California. Transpersonal psychology is the branch of psychology that includes the spiritual dimension of the individual. I interviewed Kathryn in 1995 when she was aged forty-seven.

I took my first Enlightenment Intensive in December of 1976. That Intensive was the apex of my spiritual awakening, during a time of general spiritual awakening for me. What basically happened was that I was one of those people who had a grueling time of it and not much happened until the last three hours. But then I began to have incredible experiences.

At some point around that time my energy released. It's like my voltage got amped-up to about a thousand volts. I just felt electrified, like I was plugged into a wallsocket. There were a lot of different things that happened to me while I was in that state. One of them was I began to get a lot of Christian imagery. I was raised a Protestant but never really had much religious training. I was pretty alienated from Christianity and Christian imagery. But after my energy released, it was as if the whole of reality itself became a flame, and the physical world turned into shadows. It was like what the Christian mystics talk about, the flame of God. I don't know where to locate this experience, inside or outside, but it was a huge, beautiful flame that was totally entrancing. And I looked at the physical world and it was like a shadowdance. The physical world actually appeared to be a shadowdance of the true reality, which was this incredible flame of God. I saw the illusion of life, not as an idea but as a reality. And I experienced God, not as an idea, but as a reality.

After this, every time I looked at someone, I would go into a higher consciousness. It was like a kind of light would go on, and I would see Jesus sitting in front of me. I would look at people and literally see Jesus sitting before me, both physically and in their essence. It's hard to explain this, but I'd look at a person, and suddenly there was Jesus, as tangible and as real as you or I look now. I could still see the other person's features. It was a strange amalgam. How I felt was that I was seeing Jesus in everyone. There was nothing intellectual about this at all, it was my experience of them. And I felt the spiritual passion for God in my heart for the first time. It was something I had never known before. A whole new world of possibility opened up for me then, and it has never really closed.

In one way this was really great, to see Jesus in every other, and to have experienced God. It was really great to have the grace to have these kinds of experiences. In another way it was a very shattering thing. It was a lot of new material to process. The range of experience I knew to be possible vastly expanded from this, in a short period of time. Since then I've had other types of spiritual experiences but nothing as radical as those.

INTEGRATION

Afterwards I was ambivalent about what I was going to do with these experiences. I felt these experiences weren't containable in life. This energy release I had lasted for about a month after the Intensive. I had a difficult time sleeping, I had so much energy that was running through me. I felt I had to make a choice between going into that world, the world of the flame of God, or staying in regular life. I was in a spiritual teaching at the time which taught an extreme polarization, that you had to be in one world or the other, either the world of God or the world of life, that there couldn't be a combination.

And I struggled with this for a long time, with what to do with the power of these experiences. Parts of this struggle were painful, because I wasn't ready for monastic life. I'm still not, it's really not my path. I felt, and still feel, that I have work to do, work that I feel impassioned about, in life. Yet, I had experienced something real, outside of life. I just didn't know how to fit it into my life.

I eventually went to a graduate school, the California Institute of Integral Studies, which specializes in East-West transpersonal psychology issues, and this really helped me. It mainly helped me heal the polarity of my thinking. I learned that I didn't have to polarize mystical experiences from life, I can work with them in life. I was spending a lot of time with people who considered it as holy to live in the world as to live in a monastery. I was spending time with people who had families, but who also had mystical experiences, and saw God everywhere. I realized it doesn't matter where I am.

I see that Intensive, and what I experienced there, as the seed of my work now, of what I do. I see it as the seed of my spiritual foundation. I'm always influenced by it. I'm always, in some way or another, aware of God. A door was opened with me then. And now, when I'm working with a client, even though I work with them in traditional ways, I know who I'm working with. I'm not working with just "a client." I know that we are working in a spiritual moment, a sacred moment, and I pray that what will come through me will be helpful to the person. So those experiences have really influenced me, even though I've chosen trappings that are more traditional and in life.

The main thing is that from that Intensive my view of myself and others was changed at a fundamental level. I was flooded with a whole new set of information of a different type, and a whole new kind of energy that I experienced as changing my cellular structure. I feel like a different kind of person than I was before that Intensive. I feel like an awakened person now. Everything I do, I do from that place. I have this awareness all the time, that Salinger wrote about when he saw a child pouring milk into a glass. He said he saw it as "God pouring God into God." That's how life is for me now. I'm not saying I live in this hugely enlightened state all the time, because I don't. But I do have this awareness always with me. I always have a love of God in my heart. A center of some kind, at the back of my head, is always open. I feel the interconnectedness of things all the time. And there's a kind of light I see and feel all the time. It's not as bright, like in the original experience, where everything physical fell into shadows. But somehow, some of that light is always still there for me. It's just not in front of me in the same kind of way.

So my eyes look out into the world. I'm a woman of the world, and I live in the world, but my consciousness is opened to something else at the same time. I am aware of *this dual process, always. I am an inhabitant of two worlds, and this is comfortable for me now. It wasn't comfortable for me at first, but now it is. And that is the integration of the experiences for me. I know it could change in the future, but what I've described has held pretty solid for about fifteen years now.*

DESIMIR:
ON BECOMING LESS SPIRITUAL

Desimir grew up under communism in a small village in eastern Serbia, where his relatives have lived and farmed for three hundred years. He took the first Enlightenment Intensives given in Yugoslavia in the early 1980s. Desimir spoke with me in 1995, when he was aged forty-four.

In 1980 I was studying all the spiritual and psychological books which existed in the Serbian National Library in Belgrade in that time. I studied Rudolph Steiner, dreams, health. I was doing Aikido training and Zen meditation. For five or six years I had also been practicing Transcendental Meditation for twenty minutes twice each day, in the morning and the evening.

My first impression of the name "Enlightenment Intensive," and of the idea that you can reach an enlightenment experience in three days, was that I couldn't take it seriously. From the studies I had until then, I was expecting that maybe when I am sixty or seventy, if I keep going in that direction, I can reach an enlightenment experience. But I had good contact with the people who were involved in giving the first Enlightenment Intensive in Serbia, so I thought, "Well, it is natural to go do this."

So what happened is that I didn't have a direct experience on my first Enlightenment Intensive. And I also didn't on my second. But the technique was very good for me, and I liked the work. The group atmosphere was good. And in my third Enlightenment Intensive I had the direct experience of who I am.

I remember I was sitting there, on the third day, really trying to make it. I had the impression that if I cannot get to this experience this time, then the technique doesn't work. I had the feeling that I had really done my best, I couldn't do any more. Then a little later, on a break, I was sitting there and at once I was at one with the question. I opened my eyes and looked at my hands, and I suddenly became directly conscious of myself in that moment. Of course it is not easy to explain this. It sounds ordinary, to say it like that. But I was at one with myself, in some way for the first time ever. I recognized myself, who I am, that I usually overlooked. And it was obvious to the whole group that something was happening for me. I was in a completely transformed state. I was myself, conscious of myself, presenting myself.

And an interesting thing happened after that. In that time of my life I had been doing all this spiritual work I mentioned. I realized from this experience that I was too much in those techniques, that I was splitting off from myself by doing all that stuff. How I was approaching all those practices was such that it was taking me away from the real me, actually. After this experience, I dropped a lot of those practices. So in a surprising way, the first experience of who I am actually made me less spiritual than I thought of myself before. Who I am isn't "spiritual" in that sense, it's just the real me.

I began to appreciate the method more deeply after this experience. I never found another method which provided such opportunity to find your own true knowledge and to express it. Most other systems have a theory, a dogma, a teaching that you learn about and then try to copy, or become, or somehow put into yourself. You try to make yourself be a certain way, from that. And this often leads people to become more artificial, actually. With the Enlightenment Intensive, it is the opposite. You put aside all the teachings you've gotten, and you reach for your own deeper experiences, only that. And people come into contact with their own self, and their own position in life, so they can then choose their own directions, without having to copy things outside of themselves.

I know that Enlightenment Intensives sometimes help people to become more spiritual, but for me the opposite continued to happen. As I continued to take Enlightenment Intensives and have good results, I realized even more that I should be in practical life, to operate more on a stable level, to use my spiritual experiences, and act from them, but to be on the earth more, rather than in the sky so much with spiritual things, being in some way unreal. I remember coming home from a two week Enlightenment Intensive I took, sitting in the train, feeling myself there, feeling the seat beneath me and looking at just what was around me, thinking I should act from that point, from what is really in me and around me at this moment, rather than from my ideas of where I should act from. So for me, Enlightenment Intensives brought me more to earth, to pay more attention to my family, my job, and stabilizing my money situation. For me, this is the point. Spiritual knowledge ought to make one more satisfied with oneself, having more joy in everyday things, rather than becoming more ambitious, with bigger and bigger plans. My approach for being happy in life now is that we don't need much, we can really be with what we have, and deal with it properly, and enjoy it.

JEFF:
ENLIGHTENMENT INTENSIVES AND THE EUROPEAN GROWTH MOVEMENT

Jeff Love single-handedly introduced Enlightenment Intensives into Western Europe in the early 1970s. His work has touched the lives of thousands of people, both directly and through the students he trained. I spoke with Jeff in 1996.

The first Enlightenment Intensive I gave in Europe was in 1971. It was sponsored by a growth center in London called Quaesitor. This was London's first growth center, started by Paul and Patricia Lowe. At that time they had the first group of Europeans there in a six month training program to become humanistic psychologists. There were Dutch and Germans and English, and people from other countries.

We went to a beautiful old house in Sussex and did it. I had no gong tape, I just rang the bell by hand every five minutes. Well, it was a great Enlightenment Intensive, there were a lot of breakthroughs, and it blew their minds. And this is what really kicked off my career in Europe, because these people were the first Europeans to not only be trained in humanistic psychology but to take an Enlightenment Intensive.

So they went back to their native countries: Holland, Germany, Belgium, Sweden, Norway, and they all started growth centers, because there was nothing happening in their locations. And they invited me to come give Enlightenment Intensives at their places, which I did for several years running. So for months on end I was literally going from city to city, giving an Enlightenment Intensive every weekend, in almost every country of Western Europe. I found the language barrier could be overcome by using translators, and letting people speak in their own language in the dyads. I found I could give Intensives under almost any circumstances.

My view of Enlightenment Intensives now is that they can't really solve interpersonal relationship problems directly, but they can get you in touch with who you really are, with that place that is at your center, and which is your home. And from that place, anything is possible. You can conquer your worst problems. I've seen a lot of people go through this process, and that is the main thing people get. People who experience their real self can then live from it. They don't have to worry so much about what others think. They can be who they are and go where they want with that. I actually don't know where people can go without knowing who they are. Knowing who you are is not just a benefit, it's essential to the growth process, and to whatever you do in life.

WHAT TO DO AFTER AN ENLIGHTENMENT INTENSIVE: PART II

POST-ENLIGHTENMENT INTENSIVE PRACTICES

HAKUIN EKAKU WAS A LEGENDARY ZEN MASTER who revived the ancient Rinzai school of Zen in the mid-1700s in Japan. Rinzai Zen emphasizes working on *koans* such as "What is the sound of one hand clapping?" and "What am I?" Hakuin's life and work are the subject of a number of books. In one of them, *The Essential Teachings of Zen Master Hakuin*, the author Norman Waddel writes:

> Hakuin had achieved his initial entrance into enlightenment at twenty-four, during his pilgrimage [to Zen monasteries]. In the years that followed, he had other satori experiences, "large ones and small ones, in numbers beyond count." They deepened and broadened his original enlightenment, but he still did not feel free. He was unable to integrate his realization into his ordinary life, and felt restricted when he attempted to express his understanding to others.

Well, there's a small comfort in knowing that in the 1700s there was someone who "was unable to integrate his realization into his ordinary life, and felt restricted when he attempted to express his understanding to others." This is a common experience people have to some degree following an enlightenment breakthrough.

Hakuin, we are told, kept at his *koan* practices and eventually reached a point where his search was complete; "The final decisive enlightenment that brought his long religious quest to an end," writes Waddel, "occurred on a spring night in 1726, his forty-first year."

People taking Enlightenment Intensives usually think they are doing something new and modern, something that is a part of the "growth movement" or the "New Age." They are often not aware that they are really taking part in an ancient tradition, that of truth seekers making their way toward directly experiencing the ultimate reality that lies beyond the cycles of life. Yet this is what they are doing, and they face the same issues seekers have always faced when they finally succeed in breaking through into enlightenment, however brief or illusive. After his final awakening, Hakuin urged his students to, "take the *koans* of the ancients and work into them with a single-minded determination and spirit of intense inquiry until the 'Great Death,' or breakthrough into enlightenment, is experienced. [Then] deepen and mature the initial realization through continued practice . . . so-called post-enlightenment training."

For people taking Enlightenment Intensives, what could this post-enlightenment training consist of? There are many spiritual systems available and in general terms this is what is needed for post-enlightenment training. Since there is no such follow-up system necessarily connected to the Enlightenment Intensive, and with so many options available, what people have usually done is find and follow their own paths.

However, there are some specific practices into which people who like Enlightenment Intensives seem to make an easy transition. These do not constitute a comprehensive system of growth, they are simply possible on-going practices that tend to give value to people who have developed an affinity for Enlightenment Intensives. Before outlining the specific practices here, there is a principle that underlies the whole post-enlightenment project that is helpful to grasp: *what we give our energy to, grows.*

When we give our energy to something in life, we tend to gain more understanding of that thing, and we tend to become the beneficiary of what it has to offer. It becomes bigger in our reality. For us, it seems to grow and take on significance.

This has nothing to do with moral or ethical issues; it is a simple matter of physics. If we give our energy to the TV by watching it for hours on end, our awareness and understanding of TV programs will grow, and we will be the beneficiary of what TV has to offer. TV will grow in our particular reality, and subtly influence how we are in life and where we come from when we relate.

This principle will operate anywhere we send our energy. If we keep giving our energy to paranoid thoughts, the paranoia will tend to grow, and we will be its beneficiary. If we give our energy to math, our grasp of math will grow. And so on. This principle is almost cold-hearted; it's as if it simply awaits our choice and then springs into action at our command, not making any judgments or trying to influence us one way or the other.

Similarly, if we give more of our energy to honest self-actualization and spiritual practices, if we seek relationships that support who we really are and leave behind the ones that don't, if we seek authenticity in relating, then this simple principle of physics will faithfully operate as our ally. One thing that post-enlightenment training involves is making choices that help this principle become our friend in our ability to live from the truth in life rather than just have experiences of it once in a while.

Keeping this principle in mind, what are some places to put our energy for post-enlightenment training?

CONTEMPLATION OF WHAT HAS BEEN EXPERIENCED

The first and the most natural practice is contemplating what has been directly experienced. Some days after an Enlightenment Intensive, people often think, "My experience went away," but what has really happened is that the person's mind and the distractions of our culture have come back in and swept aside what has been experienced. One gives more of one's energy to eating, talking, moving about, and getting back to regular life. Thus the elevated and purified energy state fades. But core transformative experiences can always be consciously remembered, opened up to, and drawn out, again and again, if one chooses to do this.

How to do this is simple. Spend a few minutes or so a day consciously opening up to the actuality that you experienced. If it was who you really are, open up to that. If it was of what others are, open up to that. If it was of eternal oneness, open up to that. Not so much to the memory of the experience but to the actuality now. It's as if there is a little doorway to these realms once we have experienced them, and the doorway can be opened and walked through by our simple choice to contact the actuality and open up to it. From this practice, new knowledge and abilities will arise, because these realms are the very source of divine knowledge. This practice subtly shifts how we view and regard the world. It also works with key experiences that weren't enlightenment. Troubles in the mind can't easily remain in the face of this practice, either, so there is also a calming and centering aspect. It becomes clear after a while that what was first thought to be "an experience" was really a taste of the deeper reality, which we can return to again and again, eventually emanating from that realm of deeper realness rather than merely trying to return to it.

This practice can be done under many circumstances. It isn't necessary to wait for a perfect meditative time and place. On the subway will do, as well as standing in an elevator, sitting in traffic, and so on.

AUTHENTICITY: PRESENTING YOURSELF

A compatible approach is to present yourself from what has been experienced. If you directly experienced who you are, for example, or simply got more in touch with yourself, try to express yourself more from that place, from *you* rather than from one of the usual social being-nesses of "nice," "rebellious," "shy" or whatever may be your usual habit. Communicating and taking action from whatever you experienced that was beneficial, whether a direct experience or not, brings it more into your life.

This practice is a way of showing up in life and in relationships in a more real, spontaneous way. It's the choice to cultivate being more authentic. Done well, this leads to trust in oneself. And, as Goethe put it, "As soon as you trust yourself, you will know how to live."

There may be crises resulting from this. If you realize you've been at a job or in a relationship that has nothing to do with what's true for you, then getting out can bring on a crisis. These are all personal decisions to make, but the direction is clear: if we live from the truths we've experienced rather than just remember them, they will gradually shift our lives, work, and relationships onto a more authentic and satisfying ground.

One of the forms of presenting who we are includes teaching from the experiences, either formally or informally. A lot of the reason spiritual teachers teach is to complete the experiences for themselves, to bring them to earth. Not everyone is inclined in this direction, but it can be an unusually fruitful one for those that are.

POST-ENLIGHTENMENT INTENSIVE DYADS

These include both contemplation of what has been experienced and the opportunity to express yourself from deeper, truer places. In a dyad format of forty minutes, participants respond to either of the following set of instructions:

1. "Tell me an experience you've had of yourself, life, or another, and communicate to me from its essence."

    "Thank you."

2. "Tell me an experience you've had of yourself, life, or another."

    "Thank you."

    "How have you been able to live and relate to others from this experience?"

    "Thank you."

    "What could you do to bring this experience into your life more?"

    "Thank you."

I have seen people use these dyads and recall a direct experience from an Enlightenment Intensive as long as twenty years ago. Within seconds, the essence of the experience has returned, completely undamaged by age. One sees in these moments the undying nature of direct experiences and their constant potentiality for being tapped. New knowledge and insights pour forth as if from a fountain. The question always is: will I base my life and my relating on the truths I have experienced, or on something else?

Eventually one no longer needs to use the initial experience as a referent. One no longer needs to "return" to anything. The actuality is present. In the case of the self, it's simply yourself, rather than an experience that one must return to in order to get in touch with it.

LILA GROUPS

On an Enlightenment Intensive, one contemplates a *koan*, or a question. In a Lila Group, one contemplates an answer. This is done with others, in a freestyle interchange that follows a few simple rules. This process can be very powerful.

"Lila" is a Sanskrit word meaning "divine play." In a Lila Group, five is the best number. To have the same people meeting regularly is best, assuming that everyone in the group can work together with good chemistry. At each meeting, the group decides what to contemplate. It should be a short phrase or sentence. Suppose someone took an Enlightenment Intensive and experienced that we are all the same in our true nature, or we are all connected by love, or that life is the pure relationship between divine individuals. Anything like that will be fine to use. Any phrase from scripture, or from anywhere, may be also be selected: "Do unto others as you would have them do unto you." It should just be something the group can agree on to contemplate. Then the group sits in a circle, writes the phrase down on two or three pieces of paper, and places them in the circle so people can look down and refer to them immediately.

The technique is to contemplate the statement with the intention to experience whether it is true or not and communicate what comes up. "I think the statement is bullshit and I don't believe it." Fine, everyone acknowledges that and continues contemplating. "I'm getting sleepy when I think about this." And so on. Eventually, people go deeper into the process, and remarkable insights and experiences can be had and shared. There are no turns; people just communicate when they have something to say, keeping it brief and not argumentative or attacking of someone else in the group. When someone speaks, the others just listen and acknowledge when the person is finished.

Lila Groups can become contemplative, robust, hilarious—whatever—as long as people are staying in their seats and keeping to the purpose. This is a very powerful supplemental method to the Enlightenment Intensive. It has a different flavor than does dyad work.

TRUTH GROUPS

In a Truth Group, five is also the best number, with regular meetings. The contemplation is to share the truth in the moment of oneself. Others acknowledge it. That's it.

This profoundly simple practice is a truth-walking, mindfulness process that uses the moment, the body, and the self as its endeavor. In the beginning the communications may be mind-oriented: "I'm not fully here. I'm still back in this argument I had with my mother before I came here." Barriers may also come up, "I'm feeling subtly held back, like I'm afraid of being seen. This is my usual state in life. I'm hiding here. I'm not showing you who I really am." Sometimes people have more to say, so communications should be limited to a minute or two at the most so that others have a chance. Eventually, the past and the barriers are passed through and a natural "now-ness" is entered, with many hidden pearls of simple truth for those who seek them.

Useful tips: remember to breathe. Notice the obvious about yourself. If in doubt, resort to the truth.

SCRIPTURE

Experiences of divine truth open the door to the world of scripture. A woman once told me, "I used to have this book by Krishnamurti around the house that someone had given me, and I could never understand it. But when I came home from my first Enlightenment Intensive, I went through it and found it completely inspiring."

Scripture is best read when there is some natural interest and some awareness that they are reports from other individuals who also journeyed into the realms of truth. Again, this is a personal matter and not everyone is inclined to read such writings. But it is a time-honored post-enlightenment practice that is readily available.

A very useful exercise is to return to the scripture of the religion in which you were brought up and look over it again from your own experience, as opposed to from your early education and interpretations by others.

DAILY MEDITATION

There are hundreds of options. They are known now, even in the West, to help people in numerous ways: in health, well-being, stress-reduction, creativity, effectiveness at work, capacity for love, and so on. People generally know this but often have a hard time building a daily time for meditation into their life. A daily practice can mean doing battle with the subconscious forces that keep us on the go, that refuse to let us slow down. The extremes of "I have to meditate every day" or "I never have time to do it" are also usually not our friends in this. They tend to lead to either fanaticism or a dramatized sense of guilt, both of which are forms of the ego. One thing that can help is to try to make use of some meditative time each day, and if you miss a day, don't worry about it, just begin again the next day.

I'll describe one of the most effective meditations I have found for most people who are involved in the juggling act of family, work, finances, and spiritual pursuits. It takes about five to ten minutes in the morning and five to ten minutes before going to bed. This meditation trains you to consider each day by itself at the beginning and to complete the day for yourself by reviewing it at the end. It helps you self-correct your behavior and gives you numerous aids in facing difficult decisions, people and situations. It tends to reduce the build-up of tensions and concerns that afflict modern people. It strengthens your sense of self and builds trust in your own abilities to live life well. There is no belief system or teacher to follow. It is based upon your own inner estimation and permits you to work from exactly where you are at.

MORNING MEDITATION

In the morning, after you are fully awake but before you really get going for the day, sit somewhere, preferably where you can be alone. Close your eyes and be inside.

Then anticipate the day. Just today. Let your attention go to the things you have to do today, the people you have to meet, the obligations you have, and so on. Let yourself review these. If your mind drifts off, just bring it back to today.

If you begin contemplating a larger issue or problem in your life that goes beyond today, let it occur, because it is also connected to today. It is up to you how long to contemplate it, but at a point of your choosing return to issues of just today. It is not necessary to go through the day in correct time sequence. Your attention will probably go naturally to the points of challenge first. Let it follow its own sequence.

If you have concerns about facing any situation or person, consider how to best face that situation or person. If you notice that you have a tendency to avoid something that you know you should do, determine to do it.

If there is someone with whom you are having difficulty, try to see things from that person's perspective. Then assess how to best deal with the relationship in your own estimation.

If there is any aspect of today that you have great difficulty facing, call upon assistance from a higher power, in your own way. But realize it is your job to face the issues of your life. Don't seek for any higher power to take the place of you.

When you are complete, open your eyes, rise, and meet the day.

To this basic approach, some people add aspects that are meaningful to them, such as lighting incense, using special prayers, and the like. Try to grasp the essence of what this meditation is about, and then develop a way that works for you.

EVENING MEDITATION

Before going to bed, sit alone again. Close your eyes and be inside.

Then review the day. Let your attention go over today and the things that happened, reviewing them.

Your attention will tend to go to the points that were significant to you, either negative or positive. If a point was positive, enjoy the contemplation and the reliving of it, even giving thanks.

If the point was negative, or was in your own estimation a mistake you made, let yourself go over it, digesting it, learning from it, and seeing if there is anything more to do about it.

Once you complete this process, make a choice to let the day be complete, with all its successes and failures. Let it go. Sleep in peace.

OTHER GROWTH METHODS AND EDUCATION IN THE BASICS OF LIVING

There is a wide variety of other growth methods available now. The Enlightenment Intensive, being so specialized, does not enable people to explore all the dimensions of their own growth process. Thus, people have often sought other approaches to continue this exploration. This might include bodywork, emotion work, trauma healing, shame and addiction work, and so on. It might even include aspects such as stabilizing finances or learning about health. There is a world of discovery there for people who are interested. When growth processes are used intelligently and in a balanced way, they become an important path for post-enlightenment training.

MINDFULNESS, THE ZEN OF EVERYDAY LIFE

Student: "How do you put enlightenment into life?"
Master: "By eating and by sleeping."
Student: "But everyone eats and everyone sleeps."
Master: "Yes, but not everyone eats when they eat and sleeps when they sleep."
—A well-known Zen interchange

Mindfulness, or the art of doing what you are doing and not doing what you are not doing, is a major practice in many Eastern systems. This practice of being present, of attentiveness to what one is doing, of completing one task before going on to the next, is a natural outcome of enlightenment work if one lets it be. There are deeply entrenched forces in industrialized societies that run counter to this practice, yet this practice can nonetheless be cultivated under any circumstances.

Mindfulness of the body is a similar practice that holds profound integrative potential for a seeker who has engaged in meditations of a largely mental nature. This involves spending time each day noticing what is going on in the body, letting it be, and letting the subtle energies manifest their natural healing and transforming powers. Buddha himself encouraged this practice. Mindfulness of the body, or a similar practice, is important because enlightenment in itself does not appear to automatically evolve the body. Enlightenment evolves consciousness and may open many doors of spiritual possibility. But in order to be made fully manifested it normally calls for a continuing practice of some kind that includes the body and it's energies. This is a whole field of endeavor.

Training in mindfulness techniques can be found in books in the spiritual section of many bookstores. However, they are usually best learned from a teacher. These may be found if sought.

SPIRITUAL ORIENTATION

With the initial experiences of the deeper truths of reality, one usually gains a desire to integrate these experiences into life. Eventually, though, if one goes more deeply into the realm of direct experience, this context begins to completely shift. The fabric of regular, worldly life itself begins to dissolve. Deeper direct experiences reveal to the contemplator that the apparently solid, external thing we call the physical world is an illusion, an apparentness. This has nothing to do with taking on a belief system or an "Eastern philosophy" or anything like that, it is what one actually begins to experience. One experiences, increasingly, that what we usually call life is not life, it is the Divine Other, or God. And one begins to see God in everything and everyone. When the illusion of life is thus penetrated, even for an instant, the idea of integrating experiences into it begins to go to dust. There's nothing to integrate them into. How do you integrate God into God?

Instead, one develops an ever-increasing awareness that all is God. Other terms may be used: the Divine Other; the Goddess; the Great Spirit. The term itself does not matter, what matters is the nature of the experience. This is of course a highly subjective experience. Around this point, one also begins to understand renunciation and the notion of surrender to God that people talk about. One sees the fact of it, the necessity of it in order to progress further into divine realms. It presents an enormous challenge, and also a choice.

Some people do reach this point through the Enlightenment Intensive, especially when using the two week version. It seems to me that what takes place next is a matter of predisposition. When some people stumble onto this realm of experience, they cannot deny its call. They find a path or teacher that is geared toward knowing God, and they go for it.

Others take a peek through the door into the ultimate, are inwardly transformed by the experience, and then close the door. Subjectively, something in their inner search is now fulfilled and they feel free to give their full attention to simply living life, developing a career, and so on.

Others find that a new spiritual problem has replaced whatever the old one was. For some the problem now is having one foot in one world and one foot in the other. Any choice to commit more fully to one world creates a suction effect on the foot in the other world. More involvement in worldly affairs increases the yearning for God. More involvement in spiritual practices and the godly life increases the intensity of the desires for things like children, financial security, a new car, and so on.

This is not so much a post-enlightenment practice as it is a post-enlightenment problem or opportunity, however one chooses to view it. It becomes less of a problem to the degree that one can make a choice and live with it, devoting time and energy to one realm or the other. Some go for the middle way, and to do some of both. Some do okay with this. Others feel constantly pulled in two directions. The practice here is to hack one's way through to a resolution of this issue at a personal level. It comes down to a personal journey, a personal struggle to resolve this issue of giving one's life over to the call of the divine, letting it work itself out over time.

In this respect, using the definition of what most people consider normal life, deeper enlightenment tends to destroy life and one's attachment to it. People aren't usually aware at the start that this is part of its job. It takes what we think of as life and reveals it for what it really is, God. And then it leaves us with our choice as to what to do about that. Once this issue is resolved, the spiritual problem is no longer a problem, it's simply a choice one has made.

It's beyond the job of the Enlightenment Intensive to say much more than that if one has a talent for using the method and continues to go more deeply, the tendency to regard reality in pure spiritual terms will tend to emerge, and one will be faced with the choice as to what to do about it. In the meantime, the practices outlined above are good ones to start with for people who like Enlightenment Intensive work.

THE DISSOLVING OF BEINGNESS, LEVELS OF ENLIGHTENMENT AND MISTAKEN ENLIGHTENMENT

WHAT ARE THE INNER WORKINGS of this process that take us through the jungle of our illusions and sometimes bring about an indescribable union with truth itself? "How did that happen?!" people sometimes ask after an enlightenment experience. "What was really going on?" In this chapter I will outline some of these inner workings, since a grasp of them can help lay the groundwork for a more complete integration of enlightenment experiences and for going deeper into enlightenment realms.

THE DISSOLVING OF BEINGNESSES

When someone is using the Enlightenment Technique, or any meditation technique for enlightenment, what essentially is going on is that beingnesses with which the individual has become identified are being contacted, allowed to come into awareness, and dissolved out of existence. In this process of continual de-identification, an enlightenment experience sometimes occurs.

For example, suppose I start the Enlightenment Intensive tired and stressed from overwork, and I am working on "What am I?" The beingness I'm in is one of being tired and stressed. I'm identified with it. I may not even be fully aware of how tired and stressed I really am. But when I get a sense of myself in order to intend to directly experience it, I will meet up with tiredness, stress, and what I really am, all rolled up into one ball.

As I begin to intend to directly experience what I am, and am open to what occurs, this tired, stressed beingness comes more into conscious experience. It begins to shift and loosen. As I feel it and come to know it, I begin to de-identify from it. Instead of *being* it, and looking out from it, I separate from it somewhat, causing it to come into my fuller awareness as simply tiredness and stress. In the Enlightenment Technique, my job now is to communicate it: "I am really stressed. I feel it in my arms, in my head, in my ankles even. I feel like I need a week's rest."

As I communicate about it honestly, some part of it tends to leave the space of my body and my mind. This process continues, as more and more of the beingness leaves. I don't dissolve, it does. Eventually I'm still sitting there, but the tired and stressed beingness is gone. There might be residual tiredness and stress still remaining in my body, but I am not identified with it.

This process of de-identification is at the heart of what goes on when a person works at the Enlightenment Technique, or any meditation method. Rather than a process of adding qualities, traits, or personalities to the individual in order to make him a better person, in enlightenment work the process is a more a continual shedding of what the individual is not. Understanding this can help make the process go more easily, since one can accept more that this is the very nature of the undertaking.

The foundation of the enlightenment process is that there is a "who" and "what" that one actually is. There are also many beingnesses with which we can and do become identified but which are not in themselves who and what we really are. These can be anything from tiredness and stress to what mother wanted us to be, like a good girl, for example. They can be compulsive ideas, like "I must succeed, I have to," or "I have to get everyone to like me." They may be beingnesses like "class clown," "silent wallflower," or "deep thinker." The variation is vast. And they are layered and layered upon each other. These layers of false identifications make up what we call the mind.

For example, once the tiredness and stress are gone, I may notice that I am now having concerns about my life. As I settle more into the technique, noticing what's coming up and communicating out the concerns, this beingness of concern begins to dissolve. Soon it leaves completely. I am no longer in a state of concern.

Then I may find myself in a beingness of growing bored. Many people want to quit at this stage but if one continues to experience and express the state, the beingness of being bored dissolves. And so on. Layer after layer fall away. One may go through the beingnesses of wondering, spaciness, criticalness, "nothing coming up," giddiness, suffering, whatever. These beingnesses can be strong and energetic, such as being in a particularly irritated state. They can also be subtle. Someone may come to realize, for example, that "I'm just being a good participant and a righteous seeker of truth to be better than others! It's sick! My whole search for truth is based on an attempt to prove that I'm better!" Then this too may begin to dissolve. Later, his friends might say, "Yeah, you always seemed a little too right-eous about going off to your Enlightenment Intensives like you do. Everybody's glad you're over that."

These beingnesses can be surprising. For example, being British. Normally, a British subject probably wouldn't think of "British" as being a part of his mind. First of all, there is a lot of truth to such a beingness. The man may well hold a British passport and speak with a British accent. But it is not the essential truth of who and what he is that we are looking for on the Enlightenment Intensive. Some might argue this point: "Nope, I've known Winfield for years. The old boy is British to the core, all right."

In enlightenment work we find that such a level of beingness as "British" may be solidly there, hard-wired right into the core, but it is an apparent core, not the real one. It can be commonly observed that the ancestors of many Americans came from Britain, but their progeny didn't grow up in America with a built-in British accent and some kind of innate love of cricket. The reason is that "British" is not anyone's ultimate nature. It is one possible beingness among many. The same holds true of the German beingness, the American one, the Chinese, and so on. These beingnesses are not bad, they are important for living life. For living, you have to have one. They serve as a barrier to enlightenment only when the true individual, upon hitting that layer, clings to being over-identified with them.

I remember an Enlightenment Intensive I gave in Devon, England, in 1986. A man in his fifties showed up who looked to be an English country gentleman. You don't see many of these at Enlightenment Intensives, but here he was, standing with a fine bearing, very cordial and wellspoken, all ready to go. It turned out he had a real interest in this kind of work. He sat in the dyads very properly, wearing a well-tailored tweed jacket. He gave every appearance of being British to the core. I wasn't sure how well he would take to this process. But he really went to work at the Enlightenment Technique, and on the third day he directly experienced himself as love itself. An inner light of energy and love poured forth from within him as he unselfconsciously spread his arms and presented himself as the essence of pure love. His partner could hardly believe the transformation she was seeing in front of her and she was moved to tears. The man was still British in the sense that he didn't all of a sudden lose his passport or his accent. But he looked now like some kind of glowing saint. In a tweed jacket. With a British accent. His Britishness was now completely tangential to the pure reality of his inner nature that was coming forth.

The true individual is not any beingness; it is beyond beingness, even beyond "unbeing." It is that which can be anything but which is not anything at all. There is even logic to this. If who and what we are were some *thing*, or even some "*unthing*," to the exclusion of other things or unthings, then we would not be able to be all the things that we can be, nor all the things that we can *not* be. If we were ultimately alive, for example, then we would never be able to be dead. If we were ultimately sad, then we would never be able to be happy. If we were ultimately *not* existing, we would never be able to come into existence. If we were ultimately *not* a brown-eyed man, we would never be able to be a brown-eyed man.

This process of de-identification is what accounts for the levels of enlightenment. A man experiencing himself as love itself will have touched onto a deeper aspect of his true nature than is normally experienced, but if he continues there will be further levels. These levels take a person into deeper realms of "no-thing-ness," no beingness, and even past the beingness of love, each level encompassing all levels before it and reaching to a deeper and more pure experience of the true self. For example, a beginning level of enlightenment on "What am I?" may be expressed as a profound experience that "I am." This can be subjectively very validating to the individual, especially if one touches into the eternal, undying nature of our "amness." But later, going deeper, the person may have an enlightenment experience of being "no thing" or being "everything, the entire universe itself." These stages of enlightenment can seem contradictory, but they are observable levels in the development of self-awareness of our true nature. They are the unraveling of deeper and deeper beingnesses and "unbeingnesses" with which we have become identified but that we in fact are not.

THE TRUE INDIVIDUAL, BEYOND BEINGNESS

These beingnesses tend to get more and more subtle. "I am alive." Or, "I am being here, now." Or even, "I am." At a certain stage in this work, even "I am" begins to seem like too much complication to be dragging around. When a person gets down to just "I," things are getting fairly basic, but even the notion or sense of "I" eventually gets dissolved away. Eventually, as level after level of beingness are encountered, after various levels of enlightenment are achieved, all notions and ideas of self are dissolved, and the true self remains. Our true self is indescribable: not any thing, nor any "un-thing;" not existing in time or space; and not subject to death. It is eternal, divine in nature, the source of the universe, limitless. It is sheer potentiality in a pure, total sense of the concept; all these words and the concepts that go with them fall short of the actuality and may even sound crazy, or megalomanical. Yet in enlightenment work one is drawn more deeply into this discoverable actuality.

The whole point of contemplation and meditation is to ferret out the hidden beingnesses with which we are unconsciously identified, de-identify from them, and release them. In the Enlightenment Technique, these are released through experiencing them and expressing them to the partner.

The reason a three-day Enlightenment Intensive can work in this direction is that every time there is a moment of de-identification, there is also an instantaneous opportunity for direct experience to occur. There is a crack in the system at these moments, as the true individual drops one beingness, so to speak, and climbs into another. This action normally takes place so fast that the individual doesn't notice it, although, looking back on his process with this understanding, he or she may see many places where this happened. At the moment when he drops "good boy" for example, and before he settles into, "I'm just going to say what I think," there is a crack, as it were, in the system. For an instant the individual is not fixed in anything or any unthing. Divine contact can enter. In this timeless instant, direct experience is most possible.

West returns to the East: an Enlightenment Intensive in Ahmadabad, India, 1996, mastered by Barbara Szepan.

TWO ASPECTS OF MIND

When going for enlightenment, a handy thing to know about is that there is the part of the mind that moves, and the part that doesn't.

The part that moves is the active part. This is the inner chatter and mono-logue, the part that has ideas about things. Sometimes we get into a "thinking" beingness, for example when trying to solve a math problem. We use the active part of the mind a lot in these times. This active part is what most people think of when they think of "the mind."

But there is another part of the mind that is deeper, more basic. It is the part that doesn't move. This is the basic state of being or point of view from which we view reality.

It is as if we have stuck to our face a mask, which we have forgotten about. From inside this mask we look into the active part of the mind, in which are either a lot of thoughts, some thoughts, or none, depending on the stage of contempla-tion one has reached.

This mask is the part of the mind that doesn't move. It is a fixed viewpoint. And just as a mask has a fixed expression, this fixed viewpoint will have a rigid characteristic. It might be a state of "I'm mad at life." It might be a spacy state of, "I won't be in my body, I'll be like the ether." It might be any one of thousands of possibilities, as described above. These basic beingnesses are in fact a part of the mind, and they tend to be fixed and not noticed by the contemplator. It's usually a lot easier for us to see the basic, fixed states of others than our own because our own are the ones with which we are most identified. These basic beingnesses are the place from which we contemplate. They are part of what needs to be dissolved in order for us to experience our true nature. This process also includes dissolving any fixed "unbeingness" such as "I'll never show fear" or "I won't take a position on anything, I'll just not be any point of view."

The analogy of unmasking ourselves is a good one here. But we should not try too hard at this, else an unnecessary gadget be attached to the Enlightenment Technique. In practical terms, it may just be useful to know that part of the process of working towards enlightenment involves expressing aspects of the mind that move and aspects that don't move. When contemplating on a question, this means not only to be open to those things moving in the mind but also the qualities of the very place from which the contemplation is being done. So a person might say, "There are no thoughts in my mind right now, it's empty, but I'm noticing that my basic state now is that I'm being a looker. I'm looking for who I am." Or, "There's not much coming up right now but I notice I'm in a basic state of resistance. Everything I do, I do from this state. I don't want reality to get too close to me. *GET AWAY!*" Continually applying the Enlightenment Technique, noticing the basic states and expressing them fully, tends to lead a person towards deeper de-identification and the possibility of deeper enlightenment.

MISTAKEN ENLIGHTENMENT

Sometimes people break out of an identification in spectacular fashion, rather than dissolving it quietly. Sometimes they are also deceived in this process, mistakenly thinking that a mere de-identification is enlightenment. Experienced masters can notice the difference between the two. But it can be tricky because the two conditions can look similar to the untrained observer.

For example, suppose a man is stuck in the state of "I'm sad." Suppose he has spent much of his life dramatizing that state, viewing everything that happens to him from it, and so on. And suppose that on the Enlightenment Intensive this state keeps coming up, and he finally communicates it out while working at the Enlightenment Technique.

It may happen at some point that the state will suddenly break. And he might realize in a flash, "I can be happy!" Perhaps for the first time in a very long time he lets go of the fixed state of "sad" and swings into an opposite state of, "I can be happy!"

This may be subjectively quite a revelation, quite a breakthrough. It is not enlightenment, however. It is definite progress in that now the man is unfixed from his previously entrenched state, which had him trapped and which seriously limited his ability to do the Enlightenment Technique. But this progress is not the state of union that is direct experience. Under these conditions, however, the man may believe deeply that he has had a direct experience and might even go around claiming it. He may start to think Enlightenment Intensives are great because you get to break out of being sad and you get to lighten up. Others may look at him and think, "Is that what a direct experience is?" Unfortunately in this case it is not.

To complicate matters, it is possible that in the instant of de-identification from "sad" to "happy," the man may have a genuine direct experience, although in my hypothetical example he did not. But if he had, his subjective experience would have been different. An experienced observer would have noticed a clear difference. In a direct experience, he would have experienced himself directly rather than simply gone from one state to another, neither of which is who or what he actually is.

So there is "sad," and there is "happy," and there is the true individual, which is neither of those. Who and what the individual is can be sad or happy, or a lot of other things too, but is not those states themselves.

Sometimes, in any system for enlightenment, people will mistakenly accept a de-identification for enlightenment. But these de-identifications come fundamentally from another part of the person's mind. There may be a very clear idea ('I'm happy!') and there may be a lot of enthusiasm and excitement attached to it, but it is not enlightenment. Similarly, if someone de-identifies from a suppressed energy state and experiences energy spontaneously moving in his body, causing vibrations and shakings, he or she might think this is enlightenment. Or someone might have an important insight into his or her case ("All my life I believed my mother's trip that I'm a loser, but I'm not, I can be whatever I want. This is enough enlightenment for me"). Such experiences might be important for the person but they are not in themselves enlightenment.

Hidden agendas can also bring about mistaken enlightenment experiences. Sometimes a person, having read or heard about enlightenment experiences of others, or having participated in other enlightenment programs, might generate an experience based on his ideas of what he thinks enlightenment is. Often these false experiences are due to a misguided intention: the person is subtly seeking to be someone who has had an enlightenment experience rather than actually going for the truth itself. He or she wants to be above all one of the ones who broke through and not one of the ones who didn't. This is more important than simply doing the Enlightenment Technique on honest terms and going for the truth, whatever it is.

It is a sad, flawed strategy. In these cases, the genuine search for truth gets lost in the drama of becoming acceptable. However, having acted this out, such a person may be guided back to the simple steps of the dyad process and still have a chance to get back onto the real track.

Sometimes the agenda is "I'm already enlightened." Having read or heard some teachings about how in our true nature we are already enlightened, a person might start presenting, "I'm already enlightened! There's nothing to find!" or some variation. There is truth in those words, but the words alone are not the actuality they represent. Here the person is generating a mental construct but is not in union with the reality. He is manufacturing an energy state to go with the ideas, trying to jump to the end point of enlightenment without actually facing the difficult terrain in between. These kinds of mistaken enlightenments can be a significant barrier for the person, since they come from the wrong universe. They come from the universe of "idea-land" rather than reality. Such enactments can also be distracting and confusing to others who are genuinely trying to experience the real thing.

Whether from sheer innocence or from some tragic, case-based agenda, mistaken enlightenment is sometimes a step that some people go through in any enlightenment system, ancient or modern. This is an area in which the master plays an important role. It is a major problem if an inexperienced master mistakenly accepts something as enlightenment that is not. Certainly it is a job well done when a master can successfully correct the problem and bring the person back to the real direction.

THE STEADY STATE, AND WHY ENLIGHTENMENT "GOES AWAY"

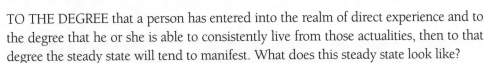

TO THE DEGREE that a person has entered into the realm of direct experience and to the degree that he or she is able to consistently live from those actualities, then to that degree the steady state will tend to manifest. What does this steady state look like?

Theoretically it means that one is always centered in the true self. It means that one is never in the mind, always in contact with what *is*. It means one would have no tendency to fall from the enlightened state and into the ripples of the mind, even in the face of life's extreme experiences such as violence, death, or even the wrath of an irate lover who knows one's innermost secrets. It means one would not get caught up in the cycles of life or try to make things be some way that they aren't. This all sounds wonderful, but is it achievable through a method such as the Enlightenment Intensive?

Not in total, not anywhere near it. My observation of people who have done well with the Enlightenment Intensive method is that this steady state is a gradually developing condition. I know of no one who, through this method alone, has achieved what could be called the final state of enlightenment: having all powers, is truly unattached, never out of touch with his or her eternal nature, and completely devoid of any residue of mind.

But I know a lot of people who over the years have strengthened their sense of who and what they are, and who are more consistently able to contact the true individual in others. These people are not exempt from the sufferings of life, but they bring a deeper self-knowledge and genuine compassion to whatever they do. The personal accounts in this book describe this development of the steady state, something which is an ongoing process for the people I interviewed.

The steady state seems to grow by plateaus. After the initial awakenings, which might be either gradual, sudden, or some combination of both, one's sense of self may grow steady in terms of who one is, but one still may see the world as somehow separate, as somehow a *thing*. Later, one's sense of the world as not separate, as not ultimately physical but rather divine in its nature, may become more stable. One may go periods of seeing the divine in all others but occasionally lose this awareness in the ordinary affairs of human life, such as at tax time. Later, this awareness may become more stable, existing under any condition. At this point it is nothing that one works at. It is simply a self-evident fact.

So it is as if we have within us a floating line, a line that when it is moved in one direction enables us to be more in touch with who we are and what is. When it floats in another direction we get more or less lost in our mind and the world of projections. There, we live from ideas, separated from what is. People have a chance on an Enlightenment Intensive to temporarily annihilate that line and delve into divine realms of direct consciousness. Afterwards, the line will normally reappear and move this way or that as the harmonics of everyday living and one's inner energy move this way and that. Sometimes, a person will deliberately re-establish the line, as in the case of someone who was experimenting into the realms of direct experience but who now prefers to put his energy into simply living life. The floating line seems to have a lot to do with the choices we make to either attend to the cultivation of applying what we have experienced or not; to choose to be either open to the actualities we have experienced or not; to be drawn into the dramas of life or not.

Often with direct experience, and because of this "floating line" situation, there is a sense of, "My enlightenment went away. Where did it go? I was in the enlightened state, but now I'm not. What happened?" Some measure of this experience is common after an Enlightenment Intensive once the high energy state falls and people return to the routines of their normal life. What is happening here, and what bearing does this have on the so-called steady state?

WHY ENLIGHTENMENT "GOES AWAY"

Strictly speaking, enlightenment doesn't go away. We go away, or appear to. Somehow we fall out of the state of direct experience without really intending to or wanting to. In a way, this is logical since, if we are honest with ourselves, we will notice that we did not manufacture the direct experience to begin with. We may have worked hard at the Enlightenment Technique and done well with it, but we did not "make" the enlightenment experience occur. It just occurred. On this point, our long-suffering egos are in a quandary: the enlightened state, being a wholly spontaneous condition of grace and not something that can be generated through the will, takes place or it does not in any given period of endeavor. We can set up conditions in which it is more likely to occur, as on the Enlightenment Intensive, but we cannot make it happen. And if we cannot make it happen, how then can we possibly make it stay?

The ego hates these realities. It has no ultimate control over whether enlightenment occurs or whether this state, once achieved, dissolves. When it is one's own ego wrestling with this situation, it can be truly exasperating, infuriating. If one happens to be a staff person on an Enlightenment Intensive, it is a little easier to observe the amazing process an ego can go through in its efforts to come to terms with its own impotency in this particular realm of reality. And just as the ego is it's own worst enemy in the project of experiencing enlightenment, so is it also its own worst enemy in trying to hang on to the enlightened state once it is there.

The basis of our fall from grace is in the fact that our ego normally continues to exist, at least in potential form. This includes all its attendant desires for things to be some way that they aren't. Most of these desires are subconscious. They continually exert a subtle force on the state of our relationship with reality. I will give an example.

A friend of mine named Daniel told me a story of a time he had an enlightenment experience on an Enlightenment Intensive back in the 1970s. Shortly after his breakthrough, he went out on one of the walking contemplations. He was in a continuing state of union and mild bliss. Everything was the way it was, and he was conscious of it and not desiring for anything to be different. There was no ego, no sense of "I'm doing this, I'm having this experience." In this low-grade *samadhi* state, which will often follow a direct experience to one degree or another, he walked around the block, marveling unself-consciously at the "is-ness" of things. But then at one point, he looked ahead and saw a shiny new sports car parked on the street. It was just sitting there, looking really cool. And before he knew what was happening, a little thought appeared in his mind, the essence of which was, "I want one of those."

Immediately, his state of grace collapsed. Suddenly things weren't completely okay the way they were. This notion of "I," together with the notion of "want," completely shattered the enlightened state before he could stop it. Suddenly he was back in the world of separation, of preferences, of "I want this and I don't want that." He was back in "I'm the doer of my acts, and the seeker after my desires."

My observation is that something like this occurs for a person every time he or she falls from the state of grace. What triggers it is usually not noticed and is usually subconscious. The only remarkable thing about Daniel's experience is that he was able to notice the process.

Of course this process will not necessarily involve an object like a car. The desire might be, "I hope I don't appear foolish by saying the things I'm saying." Or the ego may jump in and think, "Hey! I had an enlightenment experience! I did it!" Or, some subtle, desirous calculation might occur, like, "Actually, I'm more comfortable in my victim state. I'll go back to that state."

Our mind, that incredible system of points of view and desires for things to be some way or not some way, all adoringly surrounding the notion and sense of "I," is the culprit in our fall from grace. Probably it is best not to make it into too much of a bad guy, since it represents our own choices and our own particular ways of coping with a reality of which we are not fully conscious. No doubt it is wiser to try to accept its frightened and deluded attempts to cope with reality and work with them as they are, being honest about them even in their despicable ways, seeing them as extensions of our own choices.

Eventually, these falls from grace involve not only our ego but our pure choice, our choice to shut down to what is or remain open to it. This pure choice may be noticed by the individual but is usually not noticed. Usually the person just has the experience of "It went away! I'm not in the enlightened state anymore! How come?" Or, "Oh, God, my ego came up and got in the way and shattered the state before I could stop it." But underneath this experience, who and what we are has made a choice to resist the way things are. When this level is noticed, spiritual work becomes even more deep. One sees one's own divine choices and those of others, everywhere.

To come to know one's own egoistic tendencies and one's own inner choices is therefore a good follow-up practice to the Enlightenment Intensive, whether it be through an Eastern approach such as Zen practice, a Western approach such as Clearing, or other systems of mind studies. Enlightenment work goes hand-in-hand with the ongoing process of looking into the nooks and crannies of one's own system of ego, desires, and choices, those places where we force or resist how things are. In this process of purification we scrub the bowl of the mind clean and who and what we are can shine forth more steadily.

To maintain the enlightened state therefore calls for a steady condition of no ego and no residual desires, even subconscious ones. It calls for the continuous choice to be open to what is. This is a tall order. An Enlightenment Intensive creates a situation in which these conditions may be met briefly, but to bring about a situation where they are met everlastingly is beyond its capability. For that is needed a whole life context, an effective daily practice, a gradual renunciation of the pursuit of desires, and what might be called a special propensity for the endeavor. The three-day Enlightenment Intensive is an initiator into these realms rather than a tool for the full accomplishment of everything possible in enlightenment work.

However, the Enlightenment Intensive can be used for periods longer than three days, to good effect. These so-called "long Intensives" offer an opportunity for people to go more deeply with their enlightenment work and, for some, to come to know more intimately the steady state.

LONG ENLIGHTENMENT INTENSIVES: GOING DEEPER INTO THE DIVINE MYSTERIES

A LONG ENLIGHTENMENT INTENSIVE is one that lasts for more than three days. Over the years, a lot of Enlightenment Intensives lasting five days or seven days have been given, some as long as six weeks. However, the long format most often used is that of two weeks.

The two-week Enlightenment Intensive that I took in 1978 set up the conditions for me to pierce through the illusion of life and to experience for myself the face of God. The impact this event had on me was total. No part of my life went untouched: my spiritual path, my relationships, my work, and how I spent my time from then on. Afterwards, I saw every part of life and relating in spiritual terms. Whatever I have done since then has been encompassed, enfolded and shepherded by that awakening, whether I have been happy or sad, wise or foolish, or have been just doing something ordinary like watching football on TV.

Previous breakthroughs I had had were important and life-changing, especially on who I am and what I am, but somehow this, with its penetrating of life and the revealing of what I could only call God, was in another category altogether. It wasn't merely life-changing, it was life-annihilating, like being hauled from being one species of living thing into being another, one that had a new brain, new perceptions, new energy, and a radically new view of what is.

I had mainly wanted to know the truth, so I could go forward in life with some personal grasp of what's what. I was just curious, deeply so. But what I didn't realize is that any success in this project forever alters the contemplator. There is no objective research possible into these realms, no way to stay unaffected, to just know and have nothing else change. This work creates a new definition of the term "pure science," which normally implies extreme objectivity. On a two-week Enlightenment Intensive, there is some kind of pure science going on, but it increasingly becomes one of pure subjectivity rather than objectivity. This science uses the scientist's entire being and life as a laboratory. Anyone taking a long Enlightenment Intensive should be aware of this fact and accepting of it.

After five days of working hard at "What is life?" in the laboratory of myself and what is, I began to see through the flimsiness of what we normally call "life." I encountered instead our pure relationship as divine individuals. I came to know our absolute dedication to each other in love. I came to know the appropriateness, and even necessity, of service. I experienced service as one of the few forms we have that approaches expressing our true relationship with each other. I saw it grounded in how things are, not merely in belief or religious injunction or something we should do because we are guilty of sin. In the same way, I saw the underlying reality behind the teaching of renunciation; that in pure spiritual terms, renunciation is the only sensible way to deal with life, and that in fact it is necessary for developing beyond a certain point. To stumble onto these aspects of spiritual life not as beliefs but as inherent pieces of reality completely restructured my approach to reality. By the sixth day I knew that things would never be the same again for me.

I kept going deeper into this mystery I used to call life, and it kept dissolving before me. On the twelfth day I was in a dyad working with a woman who was, of all things, a former prostitute. She was now glowing before me with released internal energy, resting in a state of divine presence. And myself, purified after twelve days of intensive work, in a fairly mindless state of continual contemplation, suddenly went into union with a tiny spot on her left cheek. This spot disappeared as her cheek and revealed itself as God.

This word 'God' is something I don't like to use. But it is the best we have. It was not the concept of God that I experienced, it was It; indescribable, yet real, not fantasy. If I think about long Enlightenment Intensives and try to write about them, I cannot completely separate out my own experience from them. Sometimes when people talk about enlightenment they speak of people laughing, joyfully marveling at the oneness of things. Sometimes something like that happens. But other times, around the point where the nature of life is breached, one may not marvel at the oneness of things; rather, one may be struck dumb by what has been experienced and sit there afterward in a state of awe, pawing through the shattered remnants of what was once a fairly normal life, confronted now with an overwhelming piece of data that is both undeniable and without an instruction manual.

For myself, I went into a more or less steady state for a day and a half after that. During that time my brain felt as if it was being rewired. I was in a state of continual amazement that what holy people and religious leaders have been speaking about all these centuries really has a basis in reality to it. It's not all just delusion and blind faith.

Even though in the grand scheme of spiritual growth the experience I had was just a glimpse; even though most people do not have this kind of experience when they take a long Enlightenment Intensive; still, I was impressed by the format after this. I saw the two-week Intensive as an initiation ground of a whole other order. For anyone who finds the three-day Enlightenment Intensive as a place of coming home to something long-missed, the long Enlightenment Intensive is a naturally attractive thing and a next step to consider.

THE DESIGN DIFFERENCES

The structural features of a two-week Enlightenment Intensive have important differences from the three-day. The schedule is lighter, giving people a full eight hours' sleep. There is at least one work period every day, sometimes two, which not only provides time to take care of the physical environment but also provides a grounding to help balance all the contemplation work. People do not contemplate their question on the breaks, they cultivate a mindfulness practice of doing what they are doing and not doing what they are not doing.

WHAT HAPPENS

On a long Enlightenment Intensive, people come up against the deeper parts of their case: the more basic fixities and patterns. These are at the core of whatever struggles tend to get dramatized for a person in his or her ordinary life. These struggles could be criticalness, depression, self-loathing, suspicion of others, patterns of isolation, obsession with distractions, unconsciously setting up scenarios in which one is the victim, or some other variation. These same patterns, whatever they are, will tend to come up in concentrated forms in a long Intensive. This is natural and necessary, since these case patterns constitute the major barriers to growth.

Over a period of days in the Enlightenment Intensive format, people tend to cycle through these patterns. The pattern itself, whatever it is, begins to flower and the person more or less struggles with it, trudging on with the Enlightenment Technique. Eventually some aspect is released, and a period of clarity or a breakthrough follows. Then usually some deeper version of the same pattern will come around again. Thus, our core case patterns are purified and released layer after layer. Sometimes the core of some case pattern is extinguished altogether. All this occurs as a side effect of working at the same Enlightenment Technique used on the three-day format. Masters are called upon to give more guidance and perspective on how to go through this cycling and how to deal with the grinding through of the deeper mindstuff.

On a three-day Enlightenment Intensive, people work hard in a strong effort to break out of the mind for an instant of direct experience. What happens in longer formats is that after a few days this level of intensity can no longer be maintained. The mass of the mind seeps or pours back in and needs to be processed through. On a three-day Enlightenment Intensive it's as if, using the power of the will, a tunnel is dug through the mind so efficiently that the mind is, as it were, taken by surprise. A person can have a brief direct experience under those conditions. But once the Intensive is over and the person lays down tracks to the nearest pizza parlor, the tunnel tends to cave in. In other words, the mind comes back. But one may have had an important experience, and perhaps some part of the mind will never return.

On a long Enlightenment Intensive, it's as if the weight of the mind begins to crush in the tunnel after a few days. This weight begins to overwhelm the support beams hastily put up by the contemplator and held in place by the will. As the will weakens, so do the support beams, and more of the stones and dirt and mud of the mind pour into the tunnel through these cave-ins. One is then confronted with more material that needs carting out: memories, old stories and concerns, ancient traumas, vague intuitions with no content, stuck-viewpoints, and so on. This is sometimes a slow process, and sometimes a discouraging one. It can be discouraging to be going along in the tunnel of "What am I?" and suddenly have a major cave-in of fifteen tons of mud that one never even suspected was lurking there.

So people settle into another kind of work that is characterized by longer periods of processing, of not simply tunneling along but chewing through whole chunks of the mountain itself, with fewer or even no breakthroughs for days and days. Many people have taken a two-week Enlightenment Intensive and not broken through in the effort, although profound purification may have taken place. This pattern was noticed in Zen practice: that after the initial breakthroughs into *kensho*, there came a period of more difficult challenge for the monks, of more and deeper work to do, with fewer encouraging experiences to be had. If the monk did well at this next stage, the next level of breakthroughs eventually came, and when they did they were of a different order: deeper, more encompassing, and more transforming. But by then, the dropout rate usually had increased to the point where there were many empty cushions in the *zendo*, where once there were eager aspirants.

The long Enlightenment Intensive thus has a different purpose, in terms of emphasis, than a three-day Intensive. They are both about truth and the transformation of consciousness to a higher form. But the three-day Intensive gives total emphasis to the breakthrough into direct experience. The purpose of a long Intensive is to engage in the more basic transformation process itself, to spend time in the divine realms and steady state, and to let that change one's life how it will. This process may well include direct experiences along the way, but they are taken in stride as one continues on.

WHO ARE THEY FOR?

When I began to give long Intensives in 1981, I was somewhat crestfallen that not everyone did well on them. But I also saw it change the lives of some people so deeply, as it had mine, that I continued to give them and make changes that improved their workability. The long Enlightenment Intensive is now a true vision quest for some modern day seekers, but it also has inherent limitations and is not appropriate for some people. For those who like this style of practice, though, and have some talent for it, I always think that life is too short to miss out on the opportunity of a long Enlightenment Intensive, to see what it might hold.

Experience has shown that people who take a long Intensive should have completed at least one three-day Enlightenment Intensive and done well with it. This doesn't necessarily mean that the person has to have had a direct experience, but he or she must have settled into the format and rules comfortably and been able to progress with the Enlightenment Technique. There should be a basic affinity with this style of work, and a want to go deeper with it. The person's health should be okay, mentally, physically and emotionally. It doesn't need to be perfect, just adequate for the work. Potential participants are screened on these points prior to the Intensive. In general, people ought to be willing for their to life and how they live it to change, because day after day of this lifestyle may do that. The master should have a sense that a long Intensive is appropriate for this person.

A long Enlightenment Intensive, even more so than a three-day one, takes an adventuring spirit and a love of the journey into divine realities. This includes a willingness to face deeper barriers. There are many people who hold this longer format dear in their hearts because of what they have experienced. Looking back over many years to his first long Intensive, a man named Raphel reported:

> On the tenth day I was sitting there in a profound state of calmness and I suddenly experienced my partner directly. So much came out of this. I experienced that this other is totally worthy of my love, totally. And beautiful beyond belief. I saw with great obviousness that every other I encounter is totally worthy of my love, and my consideration. From that point on, I became the best listening partner I've ever been, because I was so engrossed in the beauty and fascination of the real other, and what they had to say.
>
> Ever since that Intensive, whenever I am with another person, I seek to go beyond the facade and relate to that other there. The secret in life is that others are really there. It's not just all this mind and facade of social relating. And there is so much beauty and fulfillment in this secret for me. I can go to the counter at the post office, and contact the postal clerk, and there's actual contact happening between me and that other. This experience of contact doesn't seem to have some goal or purpose, it's just what's real. And to be living in real contact makes my

life totally worth living. I used to think, 'What's the use of living in this body, deteriorating and then dying? Is that all there is?' Now I know that it's not all there is. What else there is, is being in contact with others, because they are what is actually there. They are what's real.

For anyone interested in a two-week Enlightenment Intensive, the place to start is to try out a three-day Enlightenment Intensive and see what it's like. If that goes well then it is worth considering taking a longer one. The two-week Enlightenment Intensive is an option. Many people who like the standard format of three days have never been drawn to go any longer. For those drawn to it, though, the longer format is now here, and waiting.

22

ENLIGHTENMENT INTENSIVES AND PSYCHOTHERAPY

ENLIGHTENMENT INTENSIVE WORK has some fundamental differences from psychotherapy. These differences are helpful to grasp for people making use of psychotherapy as well as practitioners of psychotherapeutic methods. Understanding these differences also gives much insight into how Eastern approaches to growth may be integrated with Western approaches.

Psychotherapy is defined by Webster's dictionary as "treatment of mental disorder by any of various means involving communication between a trained person and the patient and including counseling, psychoanalysis, etc." The "etc." is there because of the widely diverse and continually evolving methods now used by psychotherapists.

In the Enlightenment Intensive process, numerous doors open up along the way that offer to divert the contemplator from his or her task of enlightenment and into a psychotherapeutic process of one sort or another. When deep feelings of anger or sadness come up, for example, the person could be taken aside for a session using a technique for expressing repressed feelings. It would be an excellent opportunity, especially since therapists can spend hours trying to get a patient to actually express his or her feelings instead of just thinking and talking about them.

Similarly, if confusions come up, the person could be taken aside for some form of problem solving or counseling. If body pain or energy phenomena occurs, the person could be taken aside for a massage or another form of body work. If archetypal religious thoughts or mythical imagery come up, the person could be taken aside for Jungian analysis. If dreams occur at night, they could be analyzed for their underlying meaning. The psychotherapeutic possibilities are almost endless, because all these doorways open up regularly on Enlightenment Intensives.

By following an approach of seizing these opportunities whenever they arise, the Enlightenment Intensive could be mined for maximum psychotherapeutic results. There have in fact been incidents of untrained individuals experimenting with the Enlightenment Intensive method who have taken this very approach. Unfortunately, the cost of it is the opportunity for enlightenment, which is lost in the process. Part of the cost is also that it gives people a completely misguided idea of what enlightenment really is and what the Enlightenment Intensive is about.

On an Enlightenment Intensive, indeed in any *koan* method, the aim is to ignore or pass through any temptation to go off into other directions and instead to keep confronting the essence of reality until the question is shattered and direct experience occurs. This fact is not a negative evaluation of psychotherapy or some kind of statement that enlightenment work is somehow better. They are two different realms of activity, each an important piece of the tapestry that is the project of personal and spiritual growth.

Because of its fundamentally different purpose, the master on an Enlightenment Intensive will deliberately steer people away from psychotherapeutic endeavors. If feelings come up, the instruction will be to express them to the partner and keep seeking into, "Who is having the feeling?" If confusion comes up, the person will be instructed to communicate the confusion to the partner and keep trying to experience who it is that is confused. If body pain comes up, the person will be guided to express the body pain and keep trying to experience who it is that has the body pain. And so on. There may be variations in the instruction if the person is working on, say, "What is life," but the essential approach is always the same.

Someone familiar with psychotherapy might be concerned that this approach can make some people worse. This concern is handled in Enlightenment Intensives by two means. The first is that people with serious mental disorders are screened from participating and are referred to other methods and treatments more suitable to their condition. The second is that people with milder forms of mental disorder, such as a neurosis of one type or another (and it can be argued that almost everyone falls into this category) are normally able to get the therapeutic benefit of the communication in the dyads. Honest communication in a context of non-judgmental listening is one of the prime psychotherapeutic tools in any method, and the Enlightenment Intensive provides constant opportunity for it. As a result, most people who are interested in working on enlightenment can do so in this method, even though they may suffer from some of the milder mental ills of our culture. Their neurosis may or may not get better from taking the Enlightenment Intensive, but it shouldn't get worse.

The Enlightenment Intensive aims at an important piece of the puzzle, the essential individual. My own studies in psychotherapy came into much sharper focus once I experientially grasped the difference between the true individual and all the possible attendant avenues of exploration, which are virtually endless. Who we are is not a thought, a memory, a feeling, a body, a neurosis, a mythic image, a dream, or anything like those things. Who we are is also not some kind of composite of them, either. We can be involved with those aspects and may need to be sometimes, but they are not who we are. The direct experience of self gives an important clarification of this point and a priceless validation of who we really are. This can be deeply empowering for exploring or repairing the attendant aspects. At the same time, any given enlightenment experience doesn't necessarily annihilate a neurotic pattern. It may or it may not. I know plenty of people who have had genuine enlightenment experiences and still suffer from a life-long neurosis or have trouble getting some part of life together. Work in the realm of relationship issues, healing past traumas, or overcoming addictions, for example, almost always requires other forms of help besides simply taking more Enlightenment Intensives.

Just as I think it is a mistake for someone to go to psychotherapy to get enlightened, I also think is a mistake for someone to come to an Enlightenment

Intensive for psychotherapy. Enlightenments may occur in some psychotherapy situations, and psychotherapeutic results can occur on Enlightenment Intensives, but the methods are not primarily designed with those purposes in mind. So for efficiency's sake, I recommend that for working on enlightenment, use a method designed specifically for that. When working on psychotherapeutic issues, seek a psychotherapist.

23

FINDINGS ABOUT OUR TRUE NATURE AND THE NATURE OF LIFE

CONCLUSIONS CAN BE DRAWN about the nature of reality from what people have directly experienced on Enlightenment Intensives. When written down, these conclusions can look half-crazy, or completely crazy, as mystical experiences often do. And of course they could be wrong, or partially wrong. They certainly lose a lot in translation from experience to ideas.

However, I've had a lot of people over the years express to me what they have become directly conscious of from the state of enlightenment. Some with tears, some with ecstasy, some cautiously. They have been people from many different countries. What I have to say here is drawn partially from my own experiences but also from what these people have presented to me from their enlightenment experiences. This is what they have taught me about our reality:

There is a way that things are, a truth to reality. Reality is not all random, an illusion, or a fantasy. The questions "Who am I?" "What am I?" "What is life?" and "What is another?" are resolvable through one's own direct experience.

This truth of reality is ultimately found in who and what we really are. I don't mean us as humans that live and then die, but us in our true nature as the eternal, divine individuals we actually are. The ultimate truth, experienced directly, holds many miracles. From a human perspective this is probably the most miraculous of them all. We are the truth itself, the truth that we seek. There isn't you and me over here and the truth of reality over there. We are it, all of it. We are each intimately connected with all others.

People directly experiencing their true nature sometimes report that we are not a being or a thing existing in the cycle of life. We only appear to be those things. We are eternal, not existing in time or space, not ultimately subject to death.

Our true nature is sometimes described as sheer potential, sheer capability, in the purest, most unlimited sense of those words. Sometimes it is described as love itself. This love is eternal, absolutely unconditional. It is the love usually attributed to God. This perfect love is not somehow in us or something we must desperately get from others. It is what we are.

Sometimes our true nature is described as everything. The notion that everything exists in what we are requires a leap beyond the limits of our normal human capacity to conceive of things. But it is part of the data people sometimes report from their enlightenment experiences.

What we are is nothing and also not nothing: no where and no when, yet real, having an existence that is different from the kind we normally think of, such as that of a vase on a table. The intellect does not deal well with these kinds of paradoxes and gibberish. Sometimes our true nature is described as beyond words, beyond description.

Our true nature encompasses all the opposites of human life: good and bad, happiness and sadness, victory and defeat, and so on. As a human, with a body and personality, I at first appear to exist in the space of you, your true nature. Later it becomes clear that I do not exist in the space of you, I exist in *you*, as the eternal one that you are. You not only hold the space of all life, you *are* the space of all life. What we call 'life' is, in fact, us.

At a divine level, we appear to create this physical reality. It seems to pour forth from our what-ness in a miraculous occurrence completely beyond human logic or comprehension. From deeper experiences, however, this creation process is seen to be an illusion. Nothing is actually created or maintained or destroyed; there is only the incredible apparentness of this process, which masks the true, unchanging reality. This unchanging, eternal reality is what we are in our divine nature. Lao-tzu called it the Tao. He said it was older than God.

In our true nature we are the same, but not the same one. This is another paradox that is somehow so. People sometimes report something like, "I became one with my partner." We appear to be the same in our what-ness, and fundamentally individual in our who-ness. This makes real relating and fulfillment possible. For some of us this is a profound, life-changing realization. If we were ultimately separate and foreign to each other, no fulfillment or even meaningful relating could take place.

In a state of ignorance of our true nature, the physical world appears to be fundamentally separate and absolute in it's solidness. In the stages of awakening to our true nature, the physical world begins to appear as an aspect of our relating at a divine level. Later it it is seen as the divine itself. When union takes place, it disappears entirely and there is only the union with divine otherness. This is a subjective experience. It is not as if the trees themselves dissolve and everyone in town wonders what happened to the trees. Subjectively, for the contemplator, the trees dissolve as ultimately physical objects. They are still what they are. In relative terms, they are still "there." But now what they are is experienced as an aspect of our true nature, of the divine itself , which is to say, God.

Thus, at the beginning of the search, a table may appear separate and physical, having nothing to do with who and what we are. It may appear clearly not "divine" in any way, shape or form. As one experiences into our divine nature, though, the table is eventually experienced as something not separate from who and what we are or what God is.

A fundamental evolution seems to occur for people at the point when they directly experience that the physical world is not an ultimate reality unto itself, when it is increasingly experienced as a kind of truly magnificent cloaking device that masks our divine nature. Like those returning from a near-death experience, people after this tend to regard others as a reality more real than the physical world. They begin to regard relationship as a sacred thing, as the key to fulfillment in life. They tend to see life more and more as an ever-changing, ever-dying, incredible construct that is less important than the undying, unchanging sacredness of who and what we really are.

Normally, our enmeshment in this apparentness of life is much more entrenched than we usually think. All the ills of living, such as the suffering and the injustice, do not have an ultimate existence. But they are experienced as very real in human terms, and they call upon us to deal with them as humans. They also drive us to seek into reality much more deeply than we probably would otherwise. But these ills and sufferings of living are not somehow bigger than what we are, or more real, or more ultimate.

When people have an experience of God on an Enlightenment Intensive, the most significant point for the person is usually that this is not a belief but a reality. That alone can be a spiritually pivotal experience. Yet there is also often some quality about the nature of God that is realized in these experiences. Sometimes this is that all is forgiven; that God is love; or that we are never separate from God, only apparently so. But these realizations are never final; there always seem to be more. It may be that the infinite nature of God will provide an infinite amount of qualities so long as one continues to seek them. In this sense, God may be unknowable. Sometimes people experience themselves as God; sometimes they experience another as God. Sometimes they experience a piece of life, like a tree or a stone, as God.

Thus, all of what has been shared with me points to the conclusion that all is God, that there is nothing that is not at once both a part of God and all of God. This includes anger, betrayal, the so-called bad parts of life. This is a paradox that cannot be held easily in the mind, yet can be directly experienced. Every piece of what we see around us and within us; every relationship; every blade of grass; and every occurrence whether good or bad, is a doorway to God and the true, divine reality.

In practical terms, the truth is the transformative element, as well as the healing agent. The ills of our life embody our resistances to the way things are. They are our lies, our choices to hold out the truth, love, and otherness, in order to maintain a false sense of separation.

The truth leads to love, sooner or later, and love leads to truth. Sometimes people start out just wanting the truth, and they are surprised to eventually run into love along the way. There is a middle phase in which truth and love are seen as two sides of the same coin. Further on, truth and love become the same or, more accurately, their sameness is revealed. Again, I want to reiterate that I am not speaking from a system of thought or promoting a theory about reality. I am describing the essence of realizations from the realm of direct experience. The interwovenness of truth and love, their inherent kinship and sameness, is sometimes a spiritually profound experience for people, an experience that brings more wholeness to their life and to their contemplations.

All beauty emanates from our true nature. A sense of endless, indescribable beauty sometimes occurs on the pathway into the true nature of another. Like a lover overwhelmed by the beauty of the beloved, this inner beauty draws one, sometimes helplessly, into the universe of divine otherness.

This miracle of truth is us. It is the greatest gift we have, the pearl without price, the doorway to everything we ever wanted and more. There is a danger, though, in turning these words into another system of ideas about reality. Where the real resolution lies is in one's own practice and direct experience. This always, in the end, requires an abandonment of preconceptions, even correct ones. Anyone reading this chapter, forget about it all when you take your next Enlightenment Intensive or whatever practice you take up. Set down these ideas just as you set down this book. Seek honestly and openly into reality, so that your experiences are genuine, from the unchanging source itself.

24

WHERE TO GO TO TAKE AN ENLIGHTENMENT INTENSIVE

THE PEOPLE WHO GIVE ENLIGHTENMENT INTENSIVES work independently, which means they are scattered far and wide, and I am not in touch with all of them. It also means they work in their own style. There are, in fact, a lot of variations in how masters run their Enlightenment Intensives. Within certain limits this does not seem to reduce the effectiveness of the method. My best information is that the people listed below are trained and experienced at giving Enlightenment Intensives, and they give them in a conscientious, ethical way. However, if you are intending to take an Enlightenment Intensive, it remains your responsibility to do your own research and make your own choice about whose Enlightenment Intensive to take.

If you are a newcomer to spiritual growth work, I would generally be aware that there are sometimes untrained individuals using growth methods in unethical ways. I would come to understand the potential problems associated with power misuse, transference, counter-transference, and the emergence of cult dynamics. I would proceed with an awareness that no single method or teacher, no matter how effective or brilliant in their own right, seems to have all the answers. They are never, in the end, a substitute for the growth of self-reliant living.

At the same time I would not hold back on your interest in personal and spiritual growth if it is emerging. There is a great and honest effort afoot to develop growth techniques that truly address the many psychological ills of our culture and open the way for real spiritual evolution. Enormous contributions are coming out of this effort. The Enlightenment Intensive is part of this trend.

There are many other masters who could be on the list below; however this list provides a way to link up with the Enlightenment Intensive networks that exist in their continually evolving forms. Many of these masters will also travel if asked. They all speak English and the language of the area in which they live.

As time goes by, the contact information below will tend to become increasingly out of date. But the World Wide Web will be continually updated. To access this information use the keyword "Enlightenment Intensive." As you do this, be aware that there are many seminars available which are not Enlightenment Intensives but which use either the word 'enlightenment' or 'intensive.' Keep researching into "Enlightenment Intensive" and reading what is described, confirming that what you are finding is what is described in this book.

Bhava
1925 Juan Tabo NE
Albuquerque, New Mexico
87112 USA
800-362-5871
Website: www.swcp.com/~robicks

Patsy Saphira Boyer
3030 North 26th St.
Boise, Idaho
83702 USA
Phone: 208-342-2122
p.s.boyer@juno.com

Anna Billings
PO Box 11604
Berkeley, California
94712 USA
Phone: 510-524-0833

Ken Cadigan
PO Box 136
Paia, Hawaii
96779 USA
Phone: 808-573-3633

Edda Caraballo-Browne
8476 Friar Tuck Way
Fair Oaks, California
95628 USA
Phone: 916-962-0586
Fax: 916-442-7238

Jake Chapman
Old Manor House
The Green
Hanslope MK14 7LS
England

Enlightenment Newsletter
24 Park Avenue
Bath BA2 4QD
England
Phone: 01225-316388
EI-news@ndirect.co.uk

Rosmarie Garland
IM Toerli 6
7215 Fanas
Switzerland
Phone: 081-325-1817
Fax: 081-325-3283
rosmarie.garland@bluewin.ch

Anjali Hill
Toronto, Canada
Phone: 416-362-3368
Fax: 416-362-8796
anjaliei@aol.com

Desimir Ivanovic
Ivan Milutinovica 12/B-12
19000 Zajecar
Yugoslavia
Phone & Fax: 381-1929234

Murray Kennedy
3077 Princess Ave
North Vancouver BC
V7N 2E1 Canada
Phone: 604-984-3282

Jeff Love
12801 Graton Rd.
Sebastapol, California
95472 USA
Phone: 707-524-9394
jeff@sonic.net
lovejeff@juno.com

Peter Meadow
519 Cook St.
Farmington, Connecticut
06032 USA
Phone: 860-674-9112
Fax: 860-677-4648
pmeadow1@aol.com

Nanna Michael
Haidelweg 5
81241 Munich, Germany
Fax: 089-888-151

Lawrence Noyes
1630 North Main St. #284
Walnut Creek, California
94596 USA
Phone: 925-937-6065
ldnoyes@aol.com

Jacques de Panafieu
180 rue de Vaugirard
75015 Paris France
Fax: 33-1-46-33-92-43

Tathagata Pitaka
16140 Matilija Dr.
Los Gatos, California
95030 USA
Phone: 408-354-1987

Satyen Raja
176 Beech St.
Brampton, Ontario
L6V 1V6 Canada
Phone: 905-796-9281
Fax: 905-452-1736
beyond.brampton@mailexcite.com

Osha Reader
Origin, Star Route
Sattley, California
96124 USA
origin@mail.telis.org

Ed Riddle
Self and Other Newsletter
sao@sandoth.com
Website: www.sandoth.com

Christiane Schmelzer
Rue de Villeruse 6
1207 Geneva
Switzerland
Phone and fax: 22-735-9033
c-r-e-schmelzer@bluewin.ch

Russell Scott
RR #1
Orangeville, Ontario
L9W 2Y8 Canada
Phone: 519-942-8015
Fax: 519-942-3951

Rene Sidelsky
53 bis rue d'Alleray
75015 Paris France
Phone/fax: 01-42-50-08-54
renesy@magic.fr

SoLeiNah-Jocelyn Powe
1019-L Marron Circle NE
Albuquerque, New Mexico
87112 USA
Phone: 505-296-3712

Gudfinna Svavarsdottis
Stangarholt 5
105 Reykjavik
Iceland
Phone: 354-562-0037

Barbara Szepan
Sommegg
7215 Fanas
Switzerland
Phone: 081-325-3283
*(Contact for information about Enlightenment
Intensives in former East Germany and India)*

Keith Tarswell
1911 Bayview Ave. #302
Toronto, Ontario
M4G 3E4 Canada
Phone: 416-486-2395
ishvara@royal.net

Paul Weiss
RR1 Box 2997
Bar Harbor, Maine
06032 USA
Phone: 207-288-4246

Jack Wexler
PO Box 6
Macclesfield, SA
5153 Australia
Phone: 08-8-388-9360
jwexler@picknowl.com.au

Rita Wyser
Klosterhof 1
8630 Ruti
Switzerland
Phone & Fax: 055-240-5240
*(Also contact for information about
Enlightenment Intensives in Italy)*

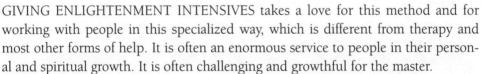

25

TRAINING TO GIVE ENLIGHTENMENT INTENSIVES

GIVING ENLIGHTENMENT INTENSIVES takes a love for this method and for working with people in this specialized way, which is different from therapy and most other forms of help. It is often an enormous service to people in their personal and spiritual growth. It is often challenging and growthful for the master.

Those interested in learning this work usually begin their training by monitoring on an Enlightenment Intensive as a staff person. The whole thing looks very different from the point of view of the staff. You become a source of support, and this can mean anything from helping out in the kitchen or the physical environment to giving your attention to the people in the dyads. Eventually, as your skills develop, it means helping people in the Enlightenment Technique and through all the stages of their process. Some people love monitoring and never hear the call to give Enlightenment Intensives. But some hear that call, and at that point, a fuller training program is needed.

The Enlightenment Masters Training Course, given through Lawrence Noyes Seminars, is a certificate program that was developed over a twenty-five-year period. The course is mostly non-residential. It includes taking and monitoring on Enlightenment Intensives, study of the training manual and other writings, completing a ten-day residential training, attending optional follow-up weekends, and giving at least five Enlightenment Intensives under consultation. Thereafter, consultation is given as necessary. Students normally take about two years to complete this program.

Student masters normally take or monitor on Enlightenment Intensives in their own area where possible, or travel to other areas if not. In the early stages of their training they sometimes organize an Enlightenment Intensive in their locality and invite a master to come and give it. The ten-day residential training is given periodically in North America, Europe, and wherever there is a demand. Continuing consultation is usually done over the phone.

During the training, all the key aspects of this work are covered. These include:

Setting up the physical environment
Screening participants
Giving the lectures and teaching the Enlightenment Technique
Learning how to run dyads
Tracking participants in their process
Handling crises and dealing with the barriers to enlightenment
Giving interviews
Going over experiences
Managing staff
Communicating about Enlightenment Intensives to the public

One of the key aspects of this training is for each master to develop his or her own style without compromising any vital component of the work. Masters learn to come from themselves, while directing and supporting people to enlightenment rather than to something else.

To inquire about training, contact Lawrence Noyes Seminars, 1630 N. Main St., Walnut Creek, CA 94596 USA. Fax: 925-934-0287; ldnoyes@aol.com.

ACKNOWLEDGMENTS

A LOT OF PEOPLE touched and influenced this book in one way or another during it's long gestation and birthing. The person most pivotal in getting the manuscript into print is Richard Handel of Bar Harbor, Maine, and Bowling Green, Virginia. Thank you, Richard, for opening the way.

The people who mastered and served on the staff of the Enlightenment Intensives I took from 1976 to 1980 provided a real service to me personally. Their good work helped form the foundation of experience that eventually led to this book. I also always appreciate the many people who have taken my Enlightenment Intensives over the years, who let me into the sacred trust of their personal and spiritual unfoldment. Again and again they inspired and heartened me by demonstrating that genuine awakening is possible in life.

My thanks to Charles Berner for his inspiration to use dyad work in *sesshin* format for the purpose of enlightenment; for developing this inspiration to a replicable form; and for the personal training he gave me.

A lot of other people have supported me and the continuation of my own work over the years. Their contact, good will and collaboration enabled me to go on. These especially include Pamela Picker, Menaka Woolford, Jeff Love, Daniel Harrison, Tara Devi, Maureen Yeomans, Nanna Michael, Sandy Villis, Peter Villis, Wolf Buntig, Osha Reader, Desimir Ivanovic, Ed Horodko, Suta Cahill, Rita Wyser, Helen Hood, Elizabeth Kock, Joyce Carlson, Dawn Nelson, Russell Scott, Anjali Hill, Judy Crawford-Smith, Dahlia Shiloh, Jacques de Panafieu, Joyce Eull, Keith

Tarswell, Anna Yeaginer, Donita Haldorson, Narada Hess, Kali Hess, Satyavati, Rosmarie Garland, John Poole, Gouri Gosslich, Ludwina Busse, and Susa Kennedy.

My special thanks to my son Shan. Without really knowing it he has been an important point of contact around which the ups and downs of writing and working could occur. My gratitude also to my mother and father for their constant supportive connection throughout my life.

I appreciate very much the help of the following friends who read parts of the manuscript and gave me their feedback, or who simply gave me advice, encouragement or solace: Judith Klinmann, Ed Riddle, Ann Zoidis, Goldie Grahame, Barry Barankin, Dawn Nelson, David Bradford, Barry Evans, Colleen Santini, Bettina Dudley, Richard Handel, Suta Cahill, and Rita Wyser.

The most inspiring part of the project for me was interviewing people about their experiences on Enlightenment Intensives. It was impossible to include more than a small part of these often lengthy and moving conversations. My thanks to all who shared themselves with me in this way.

My appreciation also to the staff at North Atlantic Books: Richard Grossinger, Emily Weinert, Nancy Koerner, and Michael Schaeffer.

Thank you all!

ABOUT THE AUTHOR

Lawrence Noyes has been lecturing and giving seminars on topics of personal and spiritual growth since 1978. From 1976–1987 he trained extensively with Charles Berner, the originator of the Enlightenment Intensive. He has given Enlightenment Intensives internationally for twenty years and has been instrumental in developing the two-week Intensives and the training course for practitioners. Noyes lives in Walnut Creek, Ca.

INDEX